Milkbar Memories

For my beautiful Gerard. It's been a tough couple of years my love, but throughout the tragedy and grief we've managed to keep each other laughing — and well fed. What more can we ask for? Here's to many more years of making memories and eating together.

Milkbar Memories

The cookbook of your childhood dreams... musk sticks, milkshakes and other fun food favourites

JANE LAWSON

MURDOCH BOOKS
SYDNEY · LONDON

Contents

Introduction

THIS BOOK HAS been squashed into a small section at the back of my brain since my first book, *Grub: Favourite Food Memories*, was published in 2007. That's almost ten years of pondering and stuffing ideas back into a cerebral drawer. Somewhere during that period I decided to make Japan my temporary home, which was without a doubt the most rewarding thing I have ever done. I fell in love with my new home Kyoto, and met the love of my life, who just happened to be a fellow Aussie. We'd still be there now if it wasn't for silly things like visas…

While I was writing my book *Zenbu Zen: Finding Food, Culture and Balance in Kyoto*, I became deeply connected to all kinds of Japanese cuisine, from the most healthy, to the crisp and comforting, to the downright challenging — but after a while I began to miss and crave certain foods from home. My humble abode, like most Japanese apartments, had no oven, which also meant there was no baking of any kind.

When we returned to Sydney I was drawn once again to the idea of writing a follow-up to *Grub*. That book was all about favourite foods from childhood that our mums and grandmothers cooked for family and friends; the kind of recipes that are often lost with the generations and rarely found in one modern compendium. My aim was to put them all in one safe place. The book was rather popular in Australia and the UK, and readers still contact me out of the blue to tell me how much they loved it and how they've bought one for every family member, and which recipes they've cooked out of it (sometimes with photos!) — often sharing food memories of their own.

While I hope people will connect as strongly with their own 'milkbar memories' as they did with their favourite family food memories, I wanted this book to be almost the opposite of homey — to include all those 'fun' foods from childhood: the stuff we ate on a Friday night when no one could be bothered cooking after work, or when mum and dad were going out for the night and takeaway was on the menu (with Tracey the cool babysitter who was heavily into KISS), the naughty stuff we snuck in on weekends when our parents weren't looking, food finds from family road trips, and the sweet icy treats we craved on summer holidays at the beach. (I probably shouldn't mention the lollies we nicked from the milkbar on our walk to school in the mornings. I blame it all on my bestie of 40 years, Vanessa — so dobbed on!) I wanted to paint a picture of freedom, mirth and frivolity, but also a connectedness to family and time spent together.

My food memories are predominantly fuelled by my dad, who was a foodie before there was a tag for such a thing. He LOVED his food, and he is without doubt responsible for my lifetime of really freakin' enjoying it and making it an important part of my career.

Unlike me, dad was very sports active, right up until his rather untimely death (he was on a golf driving range at the time). And no, it wasn't from overeating — just one of those unfortunate things. He was happy, healthy, didn't drink or smoke, ran his own business where he worked harder but shorter days than most, and spent the rest of his time living life to the fullest, which made it much easier for us when he died at 58, knowing he had managed to fit ten lives into one.

He really got a kick out of life and all its glorious parts, but one thing he was almost obsessive about was good food. Even though he couldn't cook a piece of toast, he appreciated fine cooking by others, so I was very fortunate to eat in some great restaurants from an early age, and we'd talk about the food, the flavours, the textures, how it was made and what country it came from. We formed relationships with restaurateurs, who were amused by my prematurely sophisticated palate; I'd want to know what was in that cake or salad dressing from the age of eight. Funny how these things can shape our futures.

When I was in primary school, my dad was on the road each day as a sales rep (and in the surf on either side of it), and was always excited to share his latest finds with me. If I was home from school sick (or 'chucking a sickie') he'd bring me something from the milkbar or the pie shop, and sometimes fish and chips. Often on a Friday night we'd have burgers from the Greek milkbar down the road, but when the shop changed hands and the burgers weren't up to scratch, dad went on the hunt for the best burger elsewhere in the area. He was relentless in his quest for the tastiest grub, the most pristine seafood in his fish and chips, the flakiest pie pastry, and he was rather demanding when it came to the exact amount of malt in his chocolate milkshake. Like father like daughter. On weekends, if we did our chores — and sometimes just because — we'd get 20 cents to walk up to the milkbar on the corner and buy a bag of mixed lollies. Boy, those bags seemed so full as we carefully carried our sugar bounty back down the hill; we'd have to share them with dad, of course, when we returned.

While this book might at first appear particularly 'naughty' health wise, it is less so than it could be… and I've given lots of alternative ingredients and variations along the way. Besides, I'm not suggesting you cook everything in this book at once, or eat this food on a daily basis — these are the recipes you want around for when you *do* feel like a little trip down memory lane.

Most of us are aware now that we need to exercise and eat a balance of foods, but this whole anti-sugar, anti-carb, anti-this and anti-that does my head in. I don't believe you should eliminate any one thing from your diet unless you have a medical condition — hey, none of us are built exactly the same! — but I do believe we should eat less of some things than others, and trial foods and different ways of eating until you find the right fit for you.

What concerns me most is not knowing where our food comes from, or what preservatives and chemicals are in it, how processed certain foods are, how clean the food preparation areas are, what frightening ingredients are included in certain fast foods — that kind of thing. I'm all for having a treat if you are generally eating healthily, but whether you are feeding yourself or a houseful of kids, wouldn't you rather make your own version of that particular indulgence, and know it has been made with all care, love and real ingredients? Yes, shock horror, you will find fat, sugar, dairy, carbs etc in most of these recipes (pies, fish and chips, lollies, ice creams — you know, all the stuff we sometimes crave and wish we didn't), but if you eat them in moderation or on a special occasion, what is the real harm?

I encourage you to stay away from the fast food joints, to buy organic to ensure you are taking in less chemicals generally, use less refined sugars where you can, replace dairy with an alternative natural creamy substitute if you have a lactose-intolerant person in the house, use your brain when it comes to nuts (if a child has a nut allergy, try sesame seeds or coconut in these recipes) — you know, just be reasonable and smart with your eating.

If you feel the same way, and like the idea of these treats being better for you — and often more cost effective than buying them ready-made — then you will get a lot out of this book.

If you are hosting a kiddies' party and would like the lolly bags filled with more natural sweeties, or you live in a household not wanting to shell out a small fortune for a few gourmet pies or fish and chips, or you are simply being a little more conscious about what you put into your body, then you will find this book a useful reference. Sure, it takes a little more time and energy than driving up to a window and having your food handed to you in a paper bag, but the flavour, texture and health benefits are surely worth it.

In the Milkbar chapter you'll find things like burgers, fizzy drinks, shakes, sandwiches and doughnuts — a selection of items spanning almost five decades are represented.

In Australia, just about every milkbar had a good selection of ice creams and ice blocks in their ice cream cabinet, so these icy highnesses have a dedicated chapter all of their own.

The Lolly Counter has all your old-time favourites: musk sticks, cobbers, coconut marshmallows, caramel buds, liquorice and chewy mints, to name a few.

The Pie Shop speaks for itself: savoury and sweet pies, tarts, sausage rolls, quiche…

No prizes for guessing what you'll find in the Fish 'n' Chip Shop chapter, but I've also included a wide variety of cookery methods, and a few items you'd only find in a more contemporary joint — and for those with a sweet tooth and memories as long as mine, pineapple and banana fritters!

In the Corner Store chapter you'll find home-made recipes for all those staple pantry items such as tomato, barbecue and tartare sauce, syrups for home-made fizzy drinks, shakes and ice cream treats, as well as home-made pastry, mayonnaise and even peanut butter.

Enjoy your food. It is such a big part of our existence that it really pays to appreciate and love every bite.

Chapter 1

MILK BAR

IT IS BELIEVED that Australia's first milkbar was opened in the early 1930s by a Greek immigrant known as Mick Adams (formally Joachim Tavlaridis). He opened The Black and White Milkbar in Sydney's Martin Place in quiet protest against the overconsumption of alcohol in Australia. Adams wished to offer a 'soft' option — a bar that provided lighter refreshments and specialised in milkshakes instead of booze. He may well have been disappointed to learn that some milkbars in fact became a way for people to gain access to bootleg liquor, which was then added to the milkshakes to make cocktails! His business, apparently inspired by the American-style drugstores that contained soda fountains and sundae parlours, was so extremely popular that 4000 more milkbars, mostly Greek run, are reported to have sprung up within the next five years. It is suggested that the milkbar may also have been inspired by the 'galactopoleion', a traditional Greek shop that specialised in the sale of milk products. The first milkbar was opened in the United Kingdom a few years later by a friend of Adams, and shared the same name, aesthetic and recipes as The Black and White.

By the 1970s, the prime years of my childhood, you could locate a milkbar in almost any local town or village across the land by simply finding the main drag and listening out for the hum of the refrigerator cabinet. Over the years, as convenience stores and fast-food outlets bulldozed into our worlds, the humble milkbar faded into the background.

A true milkbar is a rarity these days. Believe me, I've been looking for them. It seems that many of those that did somehow limp into this decade have only recently been pulled down to make way for progress. The handful of dinky-di milkbars that do remain tend to be in country towns or quieter suburbs, and even those just don't feel the same anymore — with much competition, they tend to be a shell of their former selves, and should be given an authentic makeover and heritage listed as far as I'm concerned!

The milkbar had everything a child could wish for. We didn't want much — it was the simple things. A visit for takeaway burgers and chips on a Friday night after mum and dad finished work and were too tired to cook was an adventure! Milkbars were pretty much the only shop you could guarantee would throw open the doors on the weekend when trading was permitted, and for a kid growing up in those times that was pretty exciting — and terribly important too. In the searing heat of a Sydney summer, when my brother and I could barely walk up the steep hill to our local shops, we did so, dragging our little bodies under a scorching sun, knowing we'd find sweet relief at the milkbar. Then we'd burn off the sugar high with a run under the sprinkler.

As a teenager, the milkbar was just as important. It sustained us with portable treats for dawn-until-dusk beach days in the summer holidays, and was an inadvertent meeting place for boys and girls — a glance in our direction from a group of young surfers playing the 'pinnies' was enough to send us into blushing fits of giggles. While the tough kids were smoking ciggies (there were always ashtrays in the milkbar), some of us thought we were just as cool by pretending to smoke lolly cigarettes, or slater-coloured vanilla cigars, or practising our bubble gum blowing technique.

As a surfer, football player and a travelling sales rep, my dad knew every milkbar from the city to the most northern tip of Sydney, and he wasn't shy about sharing his knowledge. He knew which one whizzed up the best shakes, who grilled the tastiest burgers, and who used the sweetest fruit in their pineapple crush.

My dad, a mad surfer, was a milkshake fiend. I guess that cold, sweet milky hit was perfect after a rigorous session in the ocean. He was a stickler for the choc-malted variety, and to this day it is also my favourite — although I'm partial to a good caramel shake too.

Getting the balance of flavour and texture just right in a milkshake or thickshake is key to its overall enjoyment. Keeping flavourings and ice creams as natural as possible, the way they should be, adds depth and a feel-good factor too; you'll find recipes for these throughout this book. The menu of flavours on the next two pages spans the decades of my youth, right up to today... I might be middle-aged (ergh, did I really just say that?) at this point in time, but a good milkshake instantly takes me back to my teens.

I was amused to learn through my research for this book that the original milkshakes, which were sold in Australia even before the first milkbar opened, contained no ice cream. They were a simple mix of milk, water and natural flavours, ranging from fresh and dried fruit to honey, malt, egg, butter and yeast, and were traditionally hand shaken — certainly a few steps away from what we consider a proper milkshake today.

Shake it up!

Makes 1 tall shake or 2 kid-size shakes

For milkshakes

250 ml (9 fl oz/1 cup) full-cream milk
1 large scoop ice cream

For thickshakes

170 ml (5½ fl oz/⅔ cup) full-cream milk
2–3 scoops ice cream

For smoothies

185 ml (6 fl oz/¾ cup) full-cream milk
1 large scoop ice cream

To each drink, add your desired flavouring, depending on what you're in the mood for, and how sweet or strong you like it — turn the page for inspiration!

Most of us don't have a milkshake maker at home — if you do, you'll already know how to use it. If, like me, you have to make do, simply put all the ingredients in a tall chilled container and use a stick blender to whiz everything together until well combined and frothy on top. You can also use a blender.

Pour into a chilled glass and serve with a straw.

Festival of flavours

Vanilla

VANILLA ½ teaspoon pure vanilla extract + Vanilla ice cream (page 71)

VANILLA MALTED ½ teaspoon pure vanilla extract + 1 tablespoon malt powder + Vanilla ice cream (page 71)

VANILLA SPICE ½ teaspoon pure vanilla extract + Vanilla ice cream (page 71) + 1 tablespoon malt powder + a good pinch each of ground cardamom, cinnamon and ginger

VANILLA COFFEE ¼ teaspoon pure vanilla extract + Vanilla ice cream (page 71) or Coffee ice cream (page 82) + 1–1½ tablespoons Coffee syrup (page 218)

HONEY JUMBLE ½ teaspoon pure vanilla extract + 1½ tablespoons honey + 2 teaspoons Ginger syrup (page 220) + Vanilla ice cream (page 71) + 1½ tablespoons malt powder + a large pinch of ground cinnamon

NOTE *If you use commercially made ice cream, choose a really good-quality one — it will make all the difference. Feel free to use non-dairy milk and ice cream if you prefer.*

Chocolate

CHOCOLATE 1½–2 tablespoons Chocolate syrup (page 217) + Chocolate ice cream (page 78)

CHOC HAZELNUT 2 teaspoons chocolate hazelnut spread + 1 tablespoon Chocolate syrup (page 217) + Vanilla ice cream (page 71) or Caramel hazelnut ice cream (page 96)

CHOC-MALTED 1½ tablespoons malt powder + 1½–2 tablespoons Chocolate syrup (page 217) + Vanilla ice cream (page 71)

AFTER-DINNER MINT 1 tablespoon Chocolate syrup (page 217) + 1 tablespoon Mint syrup (page 220) + Chocolate ice cream (page 78)

CHOCWORK ORANGE 1½ tablespoons Chocolate syrup (page 217) + 1½ teaspoons sweet orange marmalade + 3 teaspoons malt powder + Chocolate ice cream (page 78)

LAMINGTON 1½–2 tablespoons Chocolate syrup (page 217) + Chocolate ice cream (page 78); for dairy-free use Coconut ice cream (page 99) and use coconut milk in place of dairy milk

PEANUT BUTTER CUP 2½ teaspoons smooth peanut butter (page 221) + 2 tablespoons Chocolate syrup (page 217) + Chocolate ice cream (page 78)

CHOCOLATE BULLET 2 tablespoons Chocolate syrup (page 217) + Liquorice ice cream (page 81)

Caramel

CARAMEL ½ teaspoon pure vanilla extract + 2 tablespoons Caramel syrup (page 217) + Vanilla ice cream (page 71)

CARAMEL MALTED ½ teaspoon pure vanilla extract + 1½ tablespoons Caramel syrup (page 217) + Vanilla ice cream (page 71) + 1 tablespoon malt powder

SALTED CARAMEL 2 tablespoons Caramel syrup (page 217) + a pinch of fine sea salt + Golden caramel or Salted caramel ice cream (pages 76–77)

CREME CARAMEL 2 tablespoons Crème pâtissière (page 61) + Vanilla ice cream (page 71) + 2 tablespoons Caramel syrup (page 217)

CARAMEL HAZE 2 tablespoons Caramel syrup (page 217) + Caramel hazelnut ice cream (page 96)

CARAMEL COFFEE 1 tablespoon Caramel syrup (page 217) + 1 tablespoon Coffee syrup (page 218) + 1 tablespoon malt powder + Chocolate ice cream (page 78)

Coconut

COCONUT Use coconut milk in place of dairy milk; add Coconut ice cream (page 99) + ½ teaspoon pure vanilla extract + 1½ tablespoons Sugar syrup (page 216) or honey

COCONUT LIME Use coconut milk in place of dairy milk; add 1½ tablespoons Lime syrup (page 219), 1 tablespoon fresh lime juice + Vanilla ice cream (page 71) or Coconut ice cream (page 99)

PINE LIME DREAM Use equal quantities coconut milk and pineapple juice; add 3 teaspoons Lime syrup (page 219) + Coconut ice cream (page 99)

TROPICANA Use coconut milk in place of dairy milk; add 1½ tablespoons Passionfruit syrup (page 219) + 2 teaspoons Lime syrup (page 219) + ¼ ripe mango + 60 ml (2 fl oz/¼ cup) unsweetened pineapple juice + Vanilla ice cream (page 71) or Mango ice cream (page 99) or lychee gelato… To turn this into a cocktail, add a good splash of rum!

COCO MOJO Replace half the milk with coconut milk; add ½ teaspoon pure vanilla extract + 1–1½ tablespoons Strawberry or Raspberry syrup (page 218) + 2¼ teaspoons malt powder

Fruity

STRAWBERRY 2 tablespoons Strawberry syrup (page 218) + Vanilla ice cream (page 71) or Strawberry ice cream (page 74) or strawberry frozen yoghurt

STRAWBERRY MINT 1½ tablespoons Strawberry syrup (page 218) + ½–1 tablespoons Mint syrup (page 220) + Vanilla ice cream (page 71) or Strawberry ice cream (page 74)

STRAWBERRY SHORTCAKE 2 tablespoons Strawberry syrup (page 218) + Golden caramel ice cream (page 76) + 1½ tablespoons malt powder

PASSIONFRUIT 2 tablespoons Passionfruit syrup (page 219) + Vanilla ice cream (page 71)

PASSION TANGO Use coconut milk in place of dairy milk; add 1½ tablespoons Passionfruit syrup (page 219) + 2 teaspoons Mint syrup (page 220) + Mango ice cream (page 99)

FRUIT TART 1 tablespoon Passionfruit syrup (page 219) + 1 tablespoon Strawberry or Raspberry syrup (page 218) + Lemon ice cream (page 73)

BOOZY TRIFLE 2–3 tablespoons Crème pâtissière (page 61) or pouring custard + 2 tablespoons Strawberry syrup (page 218) + 1 tablespoon malt powder + a slug of cream sherry + Vanilla ice cream (page 71) or Strawberry ice cream (page 74)

Fresh fruit smoothies

BANANA NUT 2 teaspoons smooth peanut butter (page 221) + 1 ripe banana + 2 teaspoons malt powder + 1 tablespoon Caramel syrup (page 217) + Vanilla ice cream (page 71) or frozen yoghurt

OPEN SESAME 1 ripe banana + 3 teaspoons honey + 2 teaspoons tahini + a large pinch of ground cinnamon + Lemon ice cream (page 73) or frozen yoghurt

BERRY BLUSH 4 tablespoons mixed red berries + 1 tablespoon Strawberry or Raspberry syrup (page 218) + Strawberry ice cream (page 74) or strawberry frozen yoghurt

BLUEBERRY MAPLE 50 g (1¾ oz/⅓ cup) frozen blueberries + frozen yoghurt + 2 teaspoons maple syrup + a large pinch of ground cinnamon

FRUITY PASH 1½ tablespoons fresh passionfruit juice + ½ ripe mango + Vanilla ice cream (page 71) or Mango ice cream (page 99) or Coconut ice cream (page 99)

GOLDEN GINGER RANGA 75 g (2¾ oz/⅓ cup) fresh or bottled peach or nectarine slices + 1 tablespoon Ginger syrup (page 220) + Golden caramel ice cream (page 76) + a large pinch of freshly grated nutmeg

PEACH MELBA 75 g (2¾ oz/⅓ cup) fresh or bottled peach slices + 1 tablespoon Raspberry syrup (page 218) + 1 teaspoon lemon juice + Vanilla ice cream (page 71)

In our
neck of the woods,
thickshakes took hold in
the late 1970s when American
fast-food chains, which had put
down roots in Australian soil as early
as the late 1960s, began spreading
like the plague. In the push to be a little
'healthier', smoothies — an invention that
well and truly predated any fast-food joint
— became all the rage. They were usually
less sweet than shakes, and contained
fresh or frozen fruit blended up with
the dairy element, which was often
frozen yoghurt. Spoiler alert:
you won't find any green
smoothies here.

Pineapple crush

Every summer, on the days so super-hot it felt like your lungs were on fire, dad used to suck back these ace refreshers like nobody's business. Naturally sweet pineapple equals no added sugar... meaning these completely thirst-quenching drinks are totally healthy. I've no idea why we don't see these around nowadays — this should be our national drink.

Makes 1 large glass or 2 medium glasses

240 g (9 oz/1½ cups)
  fresh skinless
  pineapple chunks

135 g (4¾ oz/1 cup)
  ice cubes

a rounded teaspoon of
  roughly chopped mint

Put all the ingredients into a sturdy blender or food processor. Whiz until as smooth as possible. That's it!

Pour into a tall glass and serve with a wide straw — this baby is thick.

If, for some reason, your pineapple is not sweet enough, you can add a little Sugar syrup (page 216).

Totally crushing

- Add a little Lime syrup (page 219) or fresh lime juice and coconut milk.

- Add a tablespoon or two of Passionfruit syrup (page 219) for a tropical hit.

- Use chopped Mango ice cream (page 99) instead of ice, for a pine mango smoothie.

- Of course you COULD add some rum and coconut milk for cocktail hour…

I'm painfully aware that too many people drink too much fizzy stuff – soft drinks or soda pop packed with sugar, and who knows what preservatives and chemicals, and often these days, a good smack of caffeine in so-called 'energy' drinks.

If it's booze free, I'm not really a carbonated-drinks kind of gal, but occasionally on a hot and humid day, I do hanker for a tall refreshing glass of something sweet and bubbly.

While too much of anything is not a good thing, now and then a fizzy drink made with real fruit flavouring and mineral or soda water has to be better than a commercially produced version, right? So as with anything, it's best not to overdo it – but DO make sure you enjoy it.

Fizzy drinks

To make 1 glass

ice cubes

about 1½–2 tablespoons syrup of your choice;
  see pages 216–220

sparkling mineral water or soda water (club soda)

Put a few ice cubes in the bottom of a tall glass. Add the syrup of your choice, then top up with sparkling mineral water or soda water. Stir with a tall parfait spoon or swizzle stick and serve.

To make a 1 litre (35 fl oz/4 cup) bottle

about 6 tablespoons of syrup of your choice, depending how sweet you like it; see pages 216–220

1 litre (35 fl oz/4 cups) sparkling mineral water or soda water (club soda)

Pour the syrup and mineral or soda water into a jug and stir until combined. Use a funnel to pour into a 1 litre (35 fl oz/4 cup) bottle with a tightly fitting cap.

Store in the fridge. Good for a mob at home, or for taking to picnics or parties.

Create your own fizzy flavours. As a guide, use half–half or one-third of each syrup below in the recipe opposite. You'll find all the syrup recipes on pages 216–220.

Passionfruit & Lime

Passionfruit & Ginger

Coffee & Lemon

Coffee & Ginger
(+ pure vanilla extract as an optional extra)

Ginger & Lime

Ginger & Mint

Strawberry & Mint

Strawberry & Passionfruit

Strawberry, Passionfruit & Mint

Strawberry, Lime & Mint

Lemon & Ginger

Lemon, Lime & Ginger

Raspberry, Lime & Mint

Raspberry & pure vanilla extract to taste & a good pinch of cinnamon
(like a creaming soda!)

Iced coffee

My grandmother always kept a bottle of coffee syrup in a small cupboard above the kettle. I'd often walk to her house after school, picking up a Vanilla slice (page 174) or Neenish tart (page 176) on the way, and we'd sit at her kitchen table chatting while we sipped our iced coffees and shared a cake.

These days it is also popular to use a base of freshly made hot espresso coffee instead of coffee syrup, so I've included both versions here. The syrup version is sweeter and has a milder coffee flavour than the espresso, and if you store it in the fridge you'll always have it on hand, as Nana Doris did.

Iced coffee with espresso

30 ml (1 fl oz) hot espresso coffee

1 teaspoon brown sugar, or to taste

1 scoop Vanilla ice cream (page 71) or Coffee ice cream (page 82) or coffee gelato

170 ml (5½ fl oz/⅔ cup) full-cream milk

whipped cream (optional)

ground cinnamon, for sprinkling

Pour the hot espresso into a tall glass and stir in the sugar until dissolved. Add the ice cream, pour in the milk and top with whipped cream, if using. Sprinkle with ground cinnamon and serve with a long parfait spoon and a straw.

Iced coffee with coffee syrup

1½–2 tablespoons Coffee syrup (page 218)

170 ml (5½ fl oz/⅔ cup) full-cream milk

1 scoop Vanilla ice cream (page 71)

whipped cream (optional)

ground cinnamon, for sprinkling

Pour the coffee syrup into the glass, then the milk, and stir well to combine. Add the ice cream and top with whipped cream, if using. Sprinkle with ground cinnamon and serve with a long parfait spoon and straw.

Double dare you

Use a double shot of espresso coffee if you like it strong; adjust the sugar and milk to taste.

Song of Saigon

For a Vietnamese-style iced coffee, combine hot espresso coffee and condensed milk over ice.

Iced chocolate

Pour 2 tablespoons Chocolate syrup (page 217) into a tall glass, then pour in the milk and stir until well combined. Top with a scoop of Vanilla ice cream (page 71) or Chocolate ice cream (page 78), then top with whipped cream. Sprinkle with fine chocolate shavings, or sifted organic cocoa powder mixed with icing (confectioners') sugar.

Iced mocha

Use the Iced chocolate recipe above, but substitute 1 tablespoon of the Chocolate syrup with Coffee syrup (page 218).

Icy frappé

Process espresso coffee, coffee syrup and ice with some milk or ice cream until smooth.

Spider

More than just a drink with a curious name, the spider provided minutes of fun for all the family, even before reaching our lips — the best part of a spider was always the furious slurping of the overflowing creamy foam before it hit the laminated tabletop! Although known in some countries as an ice cream float, or an egg cream, here in Australia — the 'dangerous spider capital' of the world — it used to be said that the slow crazing that forms in the foam, caused by adding ice cream to carbonated liquid, resembles creeping spiders' legs. A well-known band from my youth, the Lime Spiders, were named after one of the most popular versions of this particular refreshment.

Before you start: you'll find all the ice cream recipes in the next chapter, and all the syrups in the Corner Store chapter at the back of the book.

Makes 1 tall glass

2 tablespoons syrup of your choice; see pages 216–220

1 large scoop of ice cream, in flavour of your choice; see pages 71–85

sparkling mineral water or soda water (club soda)

Put the syrup and ice cream in the base of a tall glass, mash together lightly, then top up with sparkling water. Start slurping immediately!

SPIDER MENU

Bullet
Chocolate syrup (page 217) + Liquorice ice cream (page 81)

Creaming soda
Raspberry syrup (page 218) + ½ teaspoon pure vanilla extract + a good pinch of cinnamon + Vanilla ice cream (page 71)

Lamington
Chocolate syrup (page 217) + Coconut ice cream (page 99)

Lemon, lime & bitters
Half Lemon/half Lime syrup (page 219) + dash of bitters + Vanilla ice cream (page 71)

Lemon dream
Lemon syrup (page 219) + Lemon ice cream (page 73)

Lime
Lime syrup (page 219) + Vanilla ice cream (page 71)

Mango tango
Half Lime/half Passionfruit syrup (page 219) + Mango ice cream (page 99)

Off your rocker
Chocolate syrup (page 217) + Caramel hazelnut ice cream (page 96)

Strawberries & cream
Strawberry syrup (page 218) + Vanilla ice cream (page 71)

Strawberry blonde
Ginger syrup (page 220) + Strawberry ice cream (page 74)

Pakedda chips

Aussies are rather good at stringing words together so that they sound as one. The dulcet tones of 'I'll 'av-a-packet-a chips thanks love!' inspired this somewhat exotic-sounding title for a recipe that contains only three ingredients. The plain chippies are perfectly delicious as they are, but I've included a couple of home-made flavoured salt recipes for the diehards, as I can't stand those fake flavourings in the supermarket varieties.

Makes 1 large bowl for sharing

3 large roasting or all-purpose potatoes, such as russet or dutch cream, skin on, but very well washed

mild-flavoured oil for deep-frying; I like sunflower or safflower oil

fine sea salt, for seasoning

Slice the potatoes 1–2 mm (¹⁄₁₆ inch) thick on a mandoline, or using a very sharp knife, a very steady hand and very keen eyes. (Personally, I like the fragile crunch of crisps cut to 1 mm thick — but for a sturdier chip that is better for dipping, 1.5–2 mm is perfect). If making ahead of time, keep the potato slices in a bowl of water to stop them browning, then thoroughly dry with paper towel before frying.

One-third fill a deep-fryer or large heavy-based saucepan with oil and heat to 180°C (350°F), or until a cube of bread dropped into the oil turns golden brown in 15 seconds.

Cook the chips, in batches, for about 2 minutes, or until crisp and lightly golden, stirring regularly as they cook to promote even colour and crispness. Drain well on paper towel. While still warm, sprinkle with sea salt or one of the salt variations opposite.

These chips are best served fresh, but if you need to store them, wait until they're completely cooled, then place in a couple of large snaplock bags and remove as much air as possible before sealing. Eat within a day or two.

NOTE *You can bake the chips instead of frying them. Line several baking trays with baking paper and spray with vegetable oil. Place the potato slices on top, in a single layer, and spray again. Sprinkle with fine sea salt and bake in a preheated 200°C (400°F) oven until crisp and golden.*

Salt & vinegar chips

Makes 1 large bowl for sharing

In a large non-metallic bowl, combine 750 ml (26 fl oz/3 cups) white vinegar, 250 ml (9 fl oz/ 1 cup) malt vinegar and 1½ tablespoons salt. Add your 3 large potatoes, cut into slices 1.5–2 mm (1⁄16 inch) thick, and leave to soak overnight.

Discard the liquid, dry the potato slices thoroughly, then cook as per the main recipe; they will take about 1 minute longer per batch to fry. Sprinkle with a little fine sea salt to serve if desired — they may already be salty enough for you!

Lemon, rosemary & garlic salt

Makes about 100 g (3½ oz/1⁄3 cup); enough for about 4 full batches of chips

Preheat the oven to 100°C (200°F). Line a baking tray with baking paper. In a small bowl, combine 40 g (1½ oz/1⁄3 cup) sea salt flakes, 2 tablespoons very finely grated lemon zest, the very finely chopped leaves from 2 bushy rosemary sprigs, and 6 very finely chopped garlic cloves. Mix together well, working the oils from the herbs and lemon zest into the salt. Spread out over the baking tray and leave to dry out in the oven for 1½ hours, or until you can easily crumble the lemon zest, garlic and rosemary. Leave to cool, then grind to a fine salt mixture.

Sprinkle over chips hot from the fryer as they are draining. Allow the chips to cool, so the full flavour of the salt is more pronounced.

Store in an airtight container in a cool dark place for several months; note that the flavour will fade over time.

Roast chicken salt

Makes about 100 g (3½ oz/1⁄3 cup); enough for about 4 full batches of chips

Preheat the oven to 160°C (315°F). Line a baking tray with baking paper, then scatter a few small thyme sprigs over it. Remove the skin from a small, whole chicken; use the rest of the chicken in another dish. Spread the pieces of chicken skin out flat, over the thyme, and brush lightly with melted butter. Sprinkle with sea salt, then place another sheet of baking paper over the top. Place another baking tray on top of that, then weigh it down with a small rectangular baking dish. Transfer to the oven and roast for 50–55 minutes, or until the skin is very crisp, deeply golden and glassy-looking. Drain very well on paper towel and cool.

Reduce the oven temperature to 100°C (200°F). Grind the chicken skin with 1½ tablespoons sea salt flakes, ¼ teaspoon caster (superfine) sugar, ½ teaspoon smoked paprika and ½ teaspoon onion powder, into a coarse powder. Place back on a clean, baking paper lined tray, then leave to dry out in the oven for 40 minutes. Drain again on paper towel to soak up any oil; the salt may still feel a little moist, but that's okay.

Sprinkle your roast chicken salt over chips hot from the fryer; if you let the chips cool to room temperature, the flavour of the salt will be more pronounced. This salt can also be used to season hot chips (pages 196 and 199), or chicken stews and casseroles. Store in a small airtight container in the fridge for up to a week.

Beef burger with 'The Lot'

The name speaks for itself: this burger includes every optional topping available from an authentic, old-school Aussie milkbar. The Lot. It is packed full of flavour and layered with colour and texture. However, feel free to flick the beetroot or pineapple if you aren't into it. Personally I don't dig tinned beets at any time, but I don't mind the pineapple... even on pizza — don't hate me!

PSST! *This recipe is for a classic burger, but you don't have to follow it to the letter. By all means play around with the layers — use minced lamb or pork in your patties, add pickles, relish, mayo, aïoli or chilli sauce if that floats your boat, change up your cheese choice, use other salad ingredients... you know, make it your own.*

Makes 4

500 g (1 lb 2 oz) good-quality minced (ground) beef, with decent marbling

olive oil, for pan-frying

1 small onion, finely sliced

4 pineapple rings, either fresh or tinned in natural syrup (optional)

4 streaky bacon rashers, cut in half

4 small eggs

120 g (4¼ oz) cheese (I like mild cheddar or edam for this burger), sliced 3–4 mm (³⁄₁₆ inch) thick

4 hamburger buns, split in half

softened butter, for spreading

lettuce leaves or shreds

4 slices ripe tomato

4 slices cooked beetroot (beet)

Tomato sauce (page 226) or Barbecue sauce (page 227), for drizzling

Double-crunch hot chips (page 199), to serve (optional)

Divide the beef into four equal amounts. Lightly compact each into a ball, then flatten each ball between squares of baking paper until they are about 6 mm (¼ inch) thick and 13 cm (5 inches) in diameter. They may seem large, but will shrink a little on cooking.

Heat a little oil in a large non-stick frying pan. Gently sauté the onion over medium–high heat for 10–12 minutes, or until dark golden. Remove from the pan and keep warm.

If using fresh pineapple slices, give each side a good flash over high heat in the same frying pan until they are hot through and a little charred on the edges. If using tinned pineapple, just quickly warm through on each side. Cover and keep warm.

Meanwhile put the bacon in another non-stick frying pan and cook over medium–high heat until it is as crisp as you like it, then remove from the pan and keep warm.

Cook the eggs in the bacon fat, over medium heat, until the whites are set and the yolks are still a little runny — or to your desired doneness. Remove to a warmed plate and keep warm.

Carefully wash out both frying pans. Heat your grill (broiler) to high so it is ready and waiting for your buns.

Return the clean frying pans to a fairly high heat and brush liberally with oil. When the pans are hot, season the burger patties on one side with fine sea salt and freshly cracked black pepper and cook two patties, seasoned side down, in each pan for about 80 seconds, or until well browned. Season the tops of the patties and flip them over, then top with the cheese slices and cook for a further 70 seconds. Do be careful not to cook the patties longer, as the beef can very quickly dry out. This timing yields a nice, juicy, flavoursome patty.

While the patties are cooking, pop the cut side of your burger buns under the hot grill until very lightly toasted. Butter the buns and place the bottom halves on your work surface. Top each with a little lettuce, a slice of tomato, slice of beetroot, and pineapple, if using.

As soon as the burger patties are cooked, place them, cheese side up, on top of the pineapple. Divide the sautéed onion over the patties, then top with the bacon and the eggs. Give each a good squirt of tomato or barbecue sauce and top with the bun lids.

Serve immediately, with hot chips if desired.

Crunchy chicken burger deluxe

I don't know about secret herbs and spices, but I do know a good chicken burger when I meet one. This home-made version is an absolute cracker. I understand that convenience sometimes prevails, but if your household loves a good chook burger, you need to feed them this — just be warned: there will be encore requests. Feel free to substitute plain mayonnaise for the egg salad relish.

Makes 4

4 organic chicken thigh fillets, skin off

vegetable oil, for deep-frying

4 brioche burger buns

softened butter, for spreading (optional)

butter lettuce leaves

Marinade

250 ml (9 fl oz/1 cup) buttermilk

2 garlic cloves, well bruised

2 fresh bay leaves, crumpled to release their oil

¼ teaspoon ground fennel seeds

Egg salad relish

2 hard-boiled eggs

165 g (5¾ oz/⅔ cup) Mayonnaise (page 231) or Japanese 'Kewpie' mayonnaise

1 tablespoon very finely chopped dill pickle or gherkins

1 spring onion (scallion), white part only, very finely chopped

½ teaspoon caster (superfine) sugar

2 tablespoons finely sliced chives

1 teaspoon lemon juice

Spice coating

135 g (4¾ oz/¾ cup) potato flour

½ teaspoon baking powder

1 teaspoon sweet paprika

½ teaspoon fine sea salt

½ teaspoon celery salt

½ teaspoon finely ground black pepper

a large pinch of cayenne pepper

To prepare the chicken, use a sharp knife to lightly score the fleshy underside of the thighs, where they have been cut from the bone. Beat them with the back of a rolling pin until the thicker parts have flattened out slightly.

For the marinade, combine the buttermilk, garlic, bay leaves and fennel seeds in a non-reactive bowl. Add the chicken and turn well to coat. Cover tightly with plastic wrap and marinate in the refrigerator for about 4 hours, to tenderise and flavour the meat.

Meanwhile, make the egg salad relish. Finely chop the white of one egg; eat or reserve the other egg white. Mash both the egg yolks with the mayonnaise, then place in a bowl with the chopped egg white. Add the dill pickle, spring onion, sugar and chives. Season to taste with salt, then add the lemon juice if you think it needs it. Cover and refrigerate until ready to serve.

When you're ready to cook, one-third fill a deep-fryer or large heavy-based saucepan with oil and heat to 170°C (325°F), or until a cube of bread dropped into the oil turns golden brown in 20 seconds.

In a shallow dish, combine the spice coating ingredients. Drain the chicken well, discarding the marinade. Dredge the chicken in the spice mixture on all sides, patting it on to help adhere.

Working in two batches, cook the chicken in the hot oil for 6–7 minutes, or until golden and cooked through. Drain on paper towel and keep warm in a low oven.

Butter your burger buns if desired, then top the bottom buns with lettuce, a piece of fried chicken, and a large dollop of egg salad relish. Top with the bun lids and eat.

Burger benders

Japanese karaage chicken burger

Instead of marinating the chicken thighs in a buttermilk mix, use a combination of soy sauce, mirin and sake in equal parts, and a good hit of fresh ginger and garlic — but marinate for only 30 minutes. Drain, then dust with potato flour mixed with shichimi (Japanese seven-flavour spice mix) before frying. In the egg salad, replace the sugar with mirin and add a pinch of dashi powder. Also add some sliced cucumber to the buns.

Ships ahoy, matey!

You can easily turn this into a fish burger by replacing the chicken component with a grilled fish fillet, or a piece of crumbed/battered and deep-fried fish — see the Fish 'n' Chip Shop chapter for recipes.

IF YOU'RE SUPER HARD-CORE *Leave the mayo off, butter the rolls, fill with the chicken mixture, add a drizzle of Barbecue or Tomato sauce (pages 226–227), top with finely chopped onion and grated cheese, then pop under a hot grill (broiler) until the cheese melts.*

Hot chicken rolls

My memories of hot chicken rolls are fairly sketchy, mainly because they were commonly inhaled on the way home from a big night out, ravenous after hours of podium dancing. What I do recall are flaccid white rolls with cottonball-mouthfeel filled with chicken-ish goop — inserted in white foil sleeves that made their way around an inadequate, ferris-wheel-like heating contraption. It's a miracle we never got sick... but the pre-emptive consumption of alcohol probably killed off any bugs.

I'd never buy a pre-made hot chicken roll today, but do sometimes crave the nostalgia. If you're a hot chicken roll tragic too, this is for you!

Makes 6

1 tablespoon softened butter

1 small organic chicken, about 1.2 kg (2 lb 12 oz)

sea salt flakes, for sprinkling

2 onions, peeled and halved

6 freshly baked, long soft rolls, from a good bakery

100 g (3½ oz/2 cups) finely shredded lettuce

Herbed mustard mayo

120 g (4¼ oz/½ cup) Mayonnaise (page 231), or a good-quality store-bought mayo

3 teaspoons lemon juice

a handful of flat-leaf (Italian) parsley leaves, finely shredded

a few fresh sage leaves, very finely chopped

2 spring onions (scallions), white part only, very finely chopped

½ teaspoon hot English mustard

¼ teaspoon caster (superfine) sugar

Chicken gravy

1 tablespoon plain (all-purpose) flour

310 ml (10¾ fl oz/ 1¼ cups) good-quality, hot chicken stock

1 tablespoon butter

Preheat the oven to 200°C (400°F). Using clean hands, rub the butter all over the chicken, then sprinkle with sea salt flakes. Place the four onion halves in the centre of a small roasting tin, to act as a raft for the chicken, and pop the chook on top. Pour 250 ml (9 fl oz/1 cup) water into the roasting tin. Roast for 55–60 minutes, or until the chicken is cooked through and the skin is golden.

Meanwhile, combine all the herbed mustard mayo ingredients, then cover and set aside.

When the chicken is cooked, remove it from the roasting tin, into a bowl. Lightly cover with foil and leave to rest.

Immediately place the roasting tin over two stove burners on medium–high heat. Start making the gravy by sprinkling the flour over the roasting tin and stirring well for about 1 minute. Using a small balloon whisk, gradually mix in the hot chicken stock until smooth, then keep whisking until the gravy bubbles and thickens. Whisk in the butter. Turn the heat down to low.

Remove the skin and flesh from the chicken and chop into small pieces, about 1 cm (½ inch) square. Mix about 2 cups of the chicken flesh and skin with 5–6 tablespoons of the gravy — just enough to coat it nicely; you don't want the chicken swimming in the gravy. Season to taste with sea salt and freshly ground pepper. Cover to keep warm.

Split the rolls, leaving a hinge. Liberally spread the herbed mustard mayo on the cut surfaces. Place the shredded lettuce all along the length of the rolls, then the chicken mixture. Serve straight away.

Back before we knew about the hole in the ozone layer, I was a young teen hanging at the beach, roasting my skin for hours on end, drinking milkshakes and eating burgers and chips — other things I would learn were not good for me in high doses...

In those days, the only people who ate vegie burgers were hippy surfers with dreadlocked hair and permanent tans. They drove Kombi vans, heavily perfumed with cheap cloying incense, vaguely masking the aroma of pot fumes and the bong-water-soaked shagpile comfort zone.

While a choice in vego offerings was rather slim, there was this one place in Sydney's northern beaches where even the local carnivores were throwing down the vegie burgers like they were manna from some exotic jungle heaven.

Warning: flashback-inspired recipe.

Hippy trippy vegie burger

Makes 6

olive oil, for shallow-frying

6 burger buns, or other flattish buns

Satay sauce (page 229), for drizzling

For the patties

185 g (6½ oz/1 cup) cooked green lentils

125 g (4½ oz) firm tofu

500 g (1 lb 2 oz) jap or kent pumpkin, peeled, roasted and mashed

185 g (6½ oz/1 cup) cooked brown rice

3 spring onions (scallions), chopped

2 garlic cloves, chopped

1½ teaspoons finely grated fresh ginger

½ teaspoon finely grated lemon zest

2 teaspoons curry powder

50 g (1¾ oz/1 cup) coriander (cilantro) leaves and stems, chopped

150 g (5½ oz/1 cup) plain (all-purpose) flour, plus extra for dusting

2 teaspoons fine sea salt

1 small egg

Cucumber & onion salad

2 Lebanese (short) cucumbers

2 tablespoons Japanese rice vinegar

1 teaspoon sea salt

2 teaspoons caster (superfine) sugar

½ small red onion, very finely sliced

a handful of coriander (cilantro) leaves

a handful of mint leaves

Put all the patty ingredients in a food processor and blend to combine well. Season well with sea salt and freshly ground black pepper, then chill for 1 hour.

To make the salad, use a sharp knife or a potato peeler to slice the cucumbers into ribbons 2 mm (1⁄16 inch) thick. Combine the vinegar, salt and sugar in a non-metallic bowl and add the cucumber ribbons and onion slices. Set aside for about 30 minutes, or until softened and limp. Drain, then squeeze out the excess liquid. Cover and chill until required; when ready to serve, add the coriander and mint leaves and combine well.

When you're ready to cook, heat 1.5 cm (⅝ inch) of oil in a large non-stick frying pan over medium–high heat. When the oil is hot, drop six lots of the pumpkin and lentil mixture, each about 160 g (5¾ oz/⅔ cup), into the pan and smooth out to a 1.5 cm (⅝ inch) thickness. Cook for 2–3 minutes on each side, or until golden and hot all the way through. Drain on paper towel.

Meanwhile, toast your burger buns and warm your satay sauce.

To serve, spread a little satay sauce over the bun bases. Top each with a vegie patty, then drizzle with more satay sauce. Top with a handful of the salad, then the burger lids.

Chase it all down with a wheatgrass shot, a green smoothie, or the latest health-kick juice that tastes of grass… or not.

Steak sandwich

Sometimes I prefer to keep food really simple, using the best-quality ingredients I can afford; other times I get a bit glam. Just because. So, this is a gourmet rendition of the humble steak sanger, featuring red wine caramelised onion and blue cheese. Posh, ay?

Whichever way you cut it, the building blocks to a great steak sandwich remain constant — steak, bread, onion and sauce; salad and cheese are optional. This version is what is taking my fancy right now, with more ideas over the next page for those who like to get a bit experimental. If you were after the full Aussie version, I'd point you towards the Beef Burger with 'The Lot' on page 38, and tell you to slip in a bit of steak instead of the burger patty! Go crazy.

Makes 4

3 tablespoons Mayonnaise (page 231), or a good-quality store-bought mayo

1 garlic clove, crushed

¼ teaspoon ground allspice

400 g (14 oz) beef fillet steak

1 tablespoon olive oil

8 sourdough bread slices, lightly grilled or toasted

a few large handfuls of baby English spinach leaves, or mixed salad leaves

8 thin slices of ripe tomato

80 g (2¾ oz) creamy blue cheese, or other cheese of your liking, thinly sliced

Caramelised red wine onion

1 teaspoon butter

2 teaspoons olive oil

½ teaspoon finely chopped fresh thyme

2 red onions, finely sliced

60 ml (2 fl oz/¼ cup) red wine

1 tablespoon red wine vinegar

2 teaspoons brown sugar

To caramelise the onion, melt the butter and olive oil together in a saucepan over medium–high heat. Add the thyme, onion and a large pinch of sea salt. Cook, stirring occasionally, for 10 minutes, or until the onion has softened and is lightly golden. Add the wine, vinegar and sugar, bring to the boil over high heat, then reduce to a simmer. Cook for about 30 minutes, or until the liquid has been absorbed and the onion is glossy and caramelised; during this time keep stirring regularly, to ensure it doesn't burn or stick to the pan. Cover to keep warm and set aside until ready to serve.

Combine the mayonnaise, garlic and allspice; set aside.

Slice the beef fillet into thin steaks, about 5 mm (¼ inch) thick. Season with fine sea salt and plenty of freshly cracked black pepper, pressing the pepper onto the steaks with your fingers to help it adhere.

Heat a large non-stick frying pan over high heat, then add the olive oil. When the oil is slightly smoking, add the steaks, spacing them well apart; you may need to cook them in several batches, or use two large frying pans to speed things up. Cook the steaks for 30–40 seconds on each side — you just want to sear them well, not cook them completely through, or they'll become tough. Remove to a plate and cover to keep warm.

Working quickly, spread your toasted bread slices on one side with the garlicky mayonnaise. Top with the baby spinach, the tomato slices, the steaks, the cheese and a spoonful of the onions.

Now top with the remaining slices of bread and you're good to go. A nice glass of red wouldn't go astray either.

Tokyo-a-go-go

Grilled eggplant (aubergine) slices + grilled spring onions (scallions) that have been lightly caramelised with mirin and rice vinegar + mizuna + cucumber + miso & ginger mayo. No cheese.

Ooh la lah

Pan-fried mushrooms + curly endive + Brie + chive, garlic & anchovy mayo.

Bangkok beauty

Onions caramelised with Chilli sauce (page 228), lime juice, fish sauce and palm sugar (jaggery) + cucumber ribbons + grated carrot + mint & coriander (cilantro) mayo. No cheese.

Viva España!

Season the steak with smoked paprika and salt before cooking. Add roasted red capsicum (pepper) + onions caramelised with sherry + butter lettuce + shaved Manchego cheese + Aïoli (page 231).

Oi Oi Oi

Fried egg + bacon + iceberg lettuce + cheddar cheese + Barbecue sauce (page 227).

10 Steak Sanger COMBO IDEAS

Italiano

Rocket (arugula) + tomato + Buffalo mozzarella + basil & garlic mayo.

Mexicana mama

Season the steak with ground cumin, cayenne and salt before cooking. Add avocado slices + finely sliced tomato + red onion + mild cheddar cheese + coriander (cilantro) leaves + lime, garlic & tequila mayo.

Chinese, if you please

Season the steak with ground star anise and salt before cooking. Add onions caramelised with shaoxing wine, ginger & garlic + finely shaved celery + hoisin mayo. No cheese.

Surf & turf

Add some chopped cooked prawns (shrimp) in Tartare sauce (page 230) + crisp Onion rings (page 203) + curly endive. No cheese.

It's all Greek

Onions caramelised with a splash of ouzo + baby spinach leaves + cucumber + tomato + thinly sliced feta cheese + oregano, lemon & black olive mayo.

Schnitzel sandwich
WITH COLESLAW

I'm not exactly sure why, but even today a very average schnitty or parmie (schnitzel with tomato sauce and cheese) is a crowd pleaser, although it does seem to be a bit of a boy food. I find the common chicken schnitz a bit bland, and often overcooked and dry — I prefer the juiciness and flavour of a good-quality pork schnitzel, and am happy to eat a perfectly cooked and seasoned one until the cows, er pigs, come home.

Makes 4

4 pork schnitzel steaks, about 150 g (5½ oz) each

250 ml (9 fl oz/1 cup) full-cream milk

1 garlic clove, crushed

1 wide strip of lemon zest

2 eggs

plain (all-purpose) flour, for dusting; you'll need about 250 g (9 oz)

120 g (4¼ oz/2 cups) fresh breadcrumbs

2 teaspoons very finely chopped fresh sage or rosemary

35 g (1¼ oz/⅓ cup) finely grated parmesan cheese

vegetable oil, for shallow or deep-frying

butter for spreading, if desired

8 slices of bread, or 4 flattish buns, split

Sweet-spiced coleslaw

150 g (5½ oz/2 cups) finely shredded red or green cabbage

2 teaspoons fine sea salt

2 spring onions (scallions), very finely sliced

1 small carrot, grated

1 small celery stalk, very finely sliced

120 g (4¼ oz/½ cup) Mayonnaise (page 231), or a good-quality store-bought mayo

1 tablespoon cider vinegar

½ teaspoon celery salt

1 teaspoon dijon mustard

a large pinch of ground allspice

2 teaspoons brown sugar

Beat the pork steaks with a meat mallet until they are as thin as possible — about 3 mm (⅛ inch) thick — without tearing them. Cut small nicks at even intervals around the edges so they don't curl up during frying. In a non-reactive bowl, combine the milk, garlic and lemon zest, then add the pork and turn to coat well. Cover and marinate in the refrigerator for 1 hour.

Towards the end of the marinating time, prepare your crumbing ingredients. Lightly beat the eggs in a wide bowl and set aside. Tip the flour onto a plate and season well with sea salt and freshly cracked black pepper, mixing to combine well. On another plate, combine the breadcrumbs, sage and parmesan.

Drain the schnitzels. Lightly coat each one in flour, then the egg, allowing any excess egg to drop off. Finally, coat them with the breadcrumbs, pressing down into the crumbs to help them adhere. Refrigerate for a further 1 hour.

Meanwhile, make the coleslaw. Mix the cabbage with the sea salt, really rubbing in the salt with your fingers, then let the cabbage sit in a colander for 20 minutes, or until it is a little wilted. Rinse well under running water, shake well to drain, then squeeze out handfuls of the cabbage until it is as dry as possible. Place the cabbage in a large bowl, add the spring onion, carrot and celery, and toss together. Put the remaining coleslaw ingredients in a jug and mix together well. Pour the dressing over the cabbage mixture and combine well. Cover and refrigerate until ready to serve.

If you are shallow-frying the schnitzels, heat 1 cm (½ inch) of oil in a large deep-frying pan, over medium–high heat. When the oil is hot, add the schnitzels and cook for 3–4 minutes on each side, or until golden and cooked through; you may need to cook them one at a time. Drain well on paper towel, lightly season with fine sea salt and keep warm in a low oven while cooking the remaining schnitzels.

If deep-frying the schnitzels, one-third fill a deep-fryer or large heavy-based saucepan with oil and heat to 170°C (325°F), or until a cube of bread dropped into the oil turns golden brown in 20 seconds. Cook the schnitzels for 5–6 minutes, or until golden and cooked through; you may need to cook them one at a time. Drain well on paper towel, lightly season with fine sea salt and keep warm in a low oven while cooking the remaining schnitzels.

Meanwhile, butter your bread or buns.

When all the schnitzels are cooked, fill each sandwich or bun with a schnitzel and a quarter of the coleslaw, flattening them down slightly. Cut in half to serve.

Talkin' schnitzel

Chicken schnitty

If you so desire, you can replace the pork with small chicken breasts which have been cut through the middle into two escalopes, then thinly beaten. Don't overcook!

Quick schnitzel sandwich

Do away with marinating the pork, and instead of making coleslaw, just finely shred some cabbage or lettuce and spread the bread with mayonnaise.

Veal cordon bleu schnitzel baguette

Use beaten veal escalopes. Add some thinly sliced gruyère cheese and leg ham to the top of the hot cooked schnitzel and place inside a 15 cm (6 inch) baguette which has been spread with butter or mayonnaise. Omit the coleslaw and instead add some mixed baby leaves, and some finely sliced radish and sweet white salad onion.

Not a sandwich

You can do away with the bread altogether, and make a meal of the schnitzel by serving it with the coleslaw and some boiled potatoes, potato salad, hot chips (pages 196 and 199) or wedges (page 204), or just a simple green salad.

Grilled lamb pitta wraps

The souvlaki-shop inspired wraps are my affectionate ode to the Greek-run milkbar of yesteryear. Almost every suburb had one. The influx of hardworking Greek immigrants in the 1950s introduced a whole new culture Down Under, and a certain flair and service when it came to takeaway joints and greengrocery shops.

Makes 4

1 evenly shaped eggplant (aubergine)

olive oil, for shallow-frying

4 fresh, soft, large pitta breads

Chilli sauce (page 228), for drizzling (optional)

For the lamb

2 x 220 g (7¾ oz) lamb backstraps or loin fillets

1 tablespoon chopped oregano leaves

2 large strips of lemon zest

2 teaspoons lemon juice

2 tablespoons olive oil

2 garlic cloves, well bruised

Greek salad

1 tomato, cut into 1 cm (½ inch) dice

½ small red onion, very finely sliced

1 Lebanese (short) cucumber, cut into 5 mm (¼ inch) dice

a few large handfuls of flat-leaf (Italian) parsley leaves, chopped

2 tablespoons chopped oregano leaves

2 tablespoons lemon juice

2 tablespoons olive oil

½ teaspoon ground allspice

Yoghurt sauce

130 g (4½ oz/½ cup) Greek-style yoghurt

2 garlic cloves, crushed

a squeeze of lemon juice

1 tablespoon tahini

To prepare the lamb, cut each backstrap in half, to give four squarish pieces. In a non-reactive dish, combine the oregano, lemon zest, lemon juice, olive oil and garlic. Add the lamb and turn to coat well. Cover tightly and marinate in the refrigerator for 2 hours.

Cut the eggplant lengthways into slices 5 mm (¼ inch) thick. Heat 1 cm (½ inch) olive oil in a deep-sided frying pan over medium–high heat. Working in batches, cook the eggplant, for 1 minute on each side, or until golden. Drain on paper towel and set aside.

Combine the salad ingredients in a bowl and season with salt and freshly cracked black pepper.

In a small bowl, combine the yoghurt sauce ingredients, season to taste and set aside.

Remove the lamb from the fridge to take the chill off before cooking. Meanwhile, heat a barbecue or ridged heavy-duty grill pan until very hot.

Remove the lamb from the marinade, discarding the marinade and its solids. Cook the lamb for 3–4 minutes on each side, or until well browned and just a little pink inside. Remove to a plate, cover loosely with foil and rest for 5 minutes, before slicing on a diagonal into thin slices.

While the lamb is resting, you can choose to briefly warm the pitta bread on the barbecue or under a hot grill (broiler), but don't toast it — you want it soft for wrapping.

Place your pitta breads on your work surface. Divide the yoghurt sauce among the rounds, spreading it to the edges with the back of a spoon. Place a few slices of eggplant down the centre line of each pitta, then divide the salad over the top of the eggplant. Top with a quarter of the lamb slices; drizzle the lamb with the resting juices and a little chilli sauce, if using.

Roll the pitta up tightly, then firmly wrap some baking paper or foil around, to hold it together as you eat it with your hands. Grab a couple of serviettes — you'll need them!

Chicken waldorf SALAD SANGER

The chicken waldorf salad is now my standard filling for afternoon-tea chicken sandwiches. People are always asking for the recipe, so here it is. If you're making dainty sandwiches, rather than larger rolls, simply chop everything up a little more finely. You can also use leftover roast chicken in place of the poached breasts if it makes life easier.

This wasn't by any means a standard milkbar item, but it was a damn good rendition of a chicken salad sandwich. My dad discovered these little beauties on his carpet-sales repping rounds, and whenever I was home alone from school, chucking a sickie, he'd drop in with one of these at lunchtime and make my day by sitting with me while we ate our lunch together... then he'd take off back to the road again.
Such cherished moments.

Makes 4

2 small organic chicken breasts

½ brown onion

1 bay leaf

1 clove

1 large celery stalk, plus a few celery leaves

12 g (½ oz/⅔ cup) loosely packed flat-leaf (Italian) parsley leaves

2 slender spring onions (scallions)

1 fuji or pink lady apple

1½ tablespoons lemon juice

30 g (1 oz/¼ cup) toasted walnuts

120 g (4¼ oz/½ cup) Mayonnaise (page 231), or Japanese 'Kewpie' mayonnaise

125 g (4½ oz/½ cup) sour cream

2 teaspoons dijon mustard

1 garlic clove, crushed

¼ teaspoon ground white pepper

a large pinch of freshly grated nutmeg

lettuce leaves of your choice

4 large, soft pitta bread rounds

Turn it round...

For carb curbers

Turn this dish into a simple salad for two by omitting the pitta bread rounds, slicing rather than dicing the chicken and celery, and adding some green salad leaves.

Cold turkey

Instead of using poached chicken, leftover cooked turkey breast also works well in this recipe.

Put the chicken breasts in a large saucepan, with the onion, bay leaf and clove. Cover well with water, then bring almost to the boil over medium–high heat. Turn the heat down to a simmer and poach gently for 20 minutes. Remove from the heat.

Transfer the chicken and aromatics to a bowl, then pour over enough of the cooking liquid to cover well. Cool slightly, then cover and refrigerate in the liquid until cold.

Finely dice the celery, julienne the celery leaves and parsley, and place in a large bowl. Finely slice the spring onions and add to the bowl. Cut the apple into matchsticks, mix them with 1 tablespoon of the lemon juice, then add to the bowl. Roughly chop the walnuts and add to the bowl.

Combine the mayonnaise, sour cream, mustard, garlic, white pepper, nutmeg and the remaining lemon juice, mixing well. Season with sea salt and more white pepper, to taste. Add to the bowl with the apple and vegetables.

Remove the chicken from the liquid; you can either discard the liquid, or add it to a chicken soup or stew for extra stock. Chop the chicken into 1 cm (½ inch) dice, add to the bowl of salad and combine very well. Check the seasoning again.

Wash and dry the lettuce leaves, then tear into large pieces, or shred if you prefer.

Lay your pitta breads flat on your work surface and cover with a layer of lettuce leaves. Spoon one-quarter of the chicken mixture onto each, using a spatula to spread it out evenly. Roll up the wraps, then firmly wrap a sheet of baking paper around each one to ensure the filling doesn't fall out.

Enjoy immediately. If you absolutely have to make these wraps ahead of time, please note that after 1 hour in the fridge, they will start to become quite soggy.

Cheeky SPRING ROLLS

In the 1950s a new menu item appeared, fashioned on the idea of a Chinese chicken spring roll — although since inception it has never in fact contained chicken. The original deep-fried roll combined mutton and vegetables in a slightly chewy, more robust dough wrapper — sturdy enough to handle a session at the footy or cricket, beer in hand. Today's store-bought product contains beef, but my version reclaims the chicken and spring roll wrappers, and adds some pork — hey, there are no rules, apparently! I've taken it a teensy step back towards its Chinese roots.

Makes 12

safflower or sunflower oil,
  for deep-frying

12 large square spring roll
  wrappers

1 teaspoon cornflour
  (cornstarch)

Chilli sauce (228), Tomato sauce
  (page 226), Barbecue sauce
  (page 227) or soy sauce,
  for dipping

For the filling

1 tablespoon safflower oil

200 g (7 oz) minced (ground)
  chicken thigh meat

300 g (10½ oz) minced (ground)
  pork

2 teaspoons butter

1 brown onion, very finely
  chopped

1 carrot, cut into tiny dice

1 celery stalk, cut into tiny dice

115 g (4 oz/1½ cups) very finely
  chopped cabbage

2 green beans, finely sliced

2 large garlic cloves, crushed

2½ teaspoons fine sea salt

½ teaspoon ground white pepper

1 teaspoon ground fennel seeds

½ teaspoon ground cinnamon

a good pinch of ground star
  anise

a decent pinch of ground ginger

100 g (3½ oz/½ cup) well-cooked
  pearl barley or brown rice

1 tablespoon cornflour
  (cornstarch)

375 ml (13 fl oz/1½ cups) chicken
  stock

½ teaspoon caster (superfine)
  sugar

2 teaspoons worcestershire
  sauce

To make the filling, heat 2 teaspoons safflower oil in a large frying pan. Brown the chicken and pork over medium–high heat, breaking up any lumps with the back of a fork; it should be quite crumbly. Set aside and wipe out the pan.

Add the butter and remaining safflower oil to the pan, then sauté the onion, carrot, celery, cabbage and beans over medium–high heat for about 5 minutes, or until all the ingredients are softened. Add the garlic, salt and spices, stirring well. Add the barley or rice and the chicken and pork mixture and combine well.

Mix the cornflour and chicken stock together until smooth, then add to the pan with the sugar and half the worcestershire sauce. Stir well and simmer for 15 minutes, or until the liquid has thickened. Stir in the remaining worcestershire sauce. Remove from the heat, cool slightly, then cover and refrigerate for 2 hours, or until cold.

When you're ready to cook, one-third fill a deep-fryer or large heavy-based saucepan with oil and heat to 180°C (350°F), or until a cube of bread dropped into the oil turns golden brown in 15 seconds.

Meanwhile, lay the spring roll wrappers between two lightly damp, very clean tea towels, to stop them drying out as you work. Mix the cornflour with 1½ teaspoons water, to make a thin paste.

Place one wrapper on your work surface, with a corner towards you. Shape 3 tablespoons of the filling into a log about 13 cm (5 inches) long and 4 cm (1½ inches) wide, then horizontally place it on the wrapper, about 4 cm (1½ inches) from the corner closest to you. Roll the bottom corner over the filling, tuck the ends over the filling, then roll up like a spring roll. Brush the cornflour paste on the underside of the final corner to help it adhere to the roll.

Place on a tray, cover with a lightly damp tea towel and refrigerate just until ready to cook. Repeat with the remaining filling and wrappers.

Cook two or three rolls at a time in the hot oil for 3 minutes, or until the filling is hot and the pastry golden and slightly bubbled. Drain on paper towel and keep warm in a low oven while cooking the remaining rolls.

Serve hot, with your choice of sauce for dipping.

Doughnuts

Doughnut Dan was 'the man' when I was a kid. While mum was grocery shopping, we'd press our noses to the glass window of his doughnut shop. It was a better babysitter than TV or an iPad. With precision timing, soft dough rings would swan-dive from a wide metal cone into hot oil, where they'd sizzle away over a mini mesh conveyor belt that would eventually transport the glistening rounds into waiting cinnamon sugar. The aroma was intoxicating. You couldn't walk past DD's without stopping for a bag of doughnut rings straight from the fryer. We'd always wait for the hot ones — that's when the texture and flavour are best.

Makes 24

14 g (½ oz/4 teaspoons) active dried yeast

75 g (2¾ oz/⅓ cup) caster (superfine) sugar

250 ml (9 fl oz/1 cup) lukewarm full-cream milk

600 g (1 lb 5 oz/4 cups) plain (all-purpose) flour

a pinch of sea salt

1 large egg and 2 egg yolks, lightly beaten

100 g (3½ oz) softened butter

vegetable oil, for deep-frying

Cinnamon sugar (optional)

110 g (3¾ oz/½ cup) caster (superfine) sugar

2½ tablespoons ground cinnamon

Put the yeast and about 1 teaspoon of the sugar in a small non-metallic dish. Add 80 ml (2½ fl oz/⅓ cup) of the lukewarm milk and mix together. Cover tightly with plastic wrap and set aside in a warm part of the kitchen for 15 minutes, or until foamy.

Sift the flour and salt into the bowl of an electric standing mixer fitted with a dough hook. Add the remaining sugar and mix briefly. Add the yeast mixture, egg mixture, softened butter and remaining milk. Mix at a low–medium speed until the mixture forms a dough, then increase the speed to high and mix for 6–8 minutes, or until the dough is smooth, a little shiny and elastic.

Transfer to a bowl greased with butter, then cover with a tea towel. Leave in a warm part of the kitchen for 1 hour, or until the dough has doubled in size.

Punch down the dough, then break it into 45 g (1¾ oz) pieces — use kitchen scales to weigh them, to make sure they're a uniform size. Roll each piece into a small ball and place on a tray, spaced a little apart. Cover loosely with plastic wrap and set aside again for about 15–20 minutes, or until slightly puffed.

If using cinnamon sugar to coat the doughnuts, combine the ingredients in a wide shallow container.

One-third fill a deep-fryer or large deep saucepan with oil and heat to 170°C (325°F), or until a cube of bread dropped into the oil turns golden brown in 20 seconds.

Fry the doughnuts in batches for about 3–4 minutes on each side, or until puffed, golden and cooked all the way through — open one up, and if it's still a little wet in the very centre, then cook for a further 30 seconds to 1 minute.

Remove the doughnuts from the fryer, shaking gently to remove any excess oil, then immediately roll the doughnuts over the sugar mixture, if using, to coat them well. Serve while still warm, if possible.

Doughnut fillings & GLAZES

In the 1970s there wasn't a lot of choice in doughnuts. If you didn't go for the cinnamon-sugared versions, you could pick between pink or brown icing, with or without sprinkles — or, if you were really lucky, a pineapple glazed doughnut. They all had a hole in the centre, so no fancy fillings.

These days, doughnuts have had quite a resurgence, and the ideas for filling and glazing them can be pretty eclectic. While there's something so special about a simple hot cinnamon doughnut, more decadent versions — filled with luscious, custardy crème pâtissière, or a tangy fruit curd — also float my boat. Over the next few pages you'll find enough options to concoct your own seasonal ensembles for the next decade or so.

Before filling your doughnuts with the Fresh fruit curd or Crème pâtissière recipes given here, let the doughnuts cool slightly, make an incision in their side with a small sharp knife, then insert the tip of a round-handled wooden spoon to create an air pocket inside the doughnuts.

Fresh fruit curd

Makes 1⅓ cups

80 ml (2½ fl oz/⅓ cup) strained fresh citrus juice of your choice (lemon, orange, lime, grapefruit, mandarin) OR passionfruit pulp OR sieved berry or mango purée OR puréed cooked rhubarb

1½ teaspoons finely grated citrus zest (if making a citrus curd)

75 g (2¾ oz/⅓ cup) caster (superfine) sugar, for sweeter fruits such as orange, pink grapefruit, lime, mandarin, passionfruit, strawberry or mango; or 110 g (3¾ oz/½ cup) caster sugar for more sour fruit, such as lemon, yellow grapefruit or rhubarb

125 g (4½ oz) unsalted butter

6 egg yolks, lightly beaten

Put the juice, pulp or purée in a saucepan. Add the citrus zest if using, along with the sugar and butter. Stir over medium heat until the sugar has dissolved. Remove from the heat, cool slightly and whisk in the egg yolks.

Place the pan over low heat and whisk constantly for 8 minutes, or until the curd is thick and glossy and coats the back of a spoon. It is important this mixture doesn't overheat, or it will split, so keep a good eye on it.

Remove from the heat and pour into a bowl. Cool slightly, then place a piece of baking paper or plastic wrap directly over the surface, to prevent a skin forming. Refrigerate until cold before using. (If you find the curd too sweet or tart, mix some whipped cream through it.)

Crème pâtissière
(vanilla pastry cream)

Makes 2½ cups

375 ml (13 fl oz/1½ cups) thin (pouring) cream

125 ml (4 fl oz/½ cup) full-cream milk

7 egg yolks

75 g (2¾ oz/⅓ cup) caster (superfine) sugar

1½ teaspoons pure vanilla extract

2 tablespoons plain (all-purpose) flour

1½ tablespoons cornflour (cornstarch)

Gently heat the cream and milk in a saucepan over medium heat until it comes almost to the boil. Remove from the heat.

Meanwhile, in a bowl, whisk together the egg yolks, sugar, vanilla, flour and cornflour until smooth.

Constantly whisking, gradually pour the warm milk mixture into the egg mixture.

Pour into a clean, heavy-based saucepan and stir over low heat for 15 minutes, or until the custard is very thick and smooth.

Remove from the heat, pour into a bowl and cover with a sheet of baking paper, pressing it down directly onto the surface of the custard to prevent a skin forming.

Refrigerate for 3–4 hours, or until completely cold.

Crème pâtissière delights

Chocolate

Reduce the vanilla to just 1 teaspoon. Stir 150 g (5½ oz) grated dark chocolate into the custard in the last minutes of cooking; when you remove it from the heat, keep whisking until the chocolate has melted and the custard has an even colour.

Coconut

Replace the dairy cream and milk with 250 ml (9 fl oz/1 cup) coconut cream and 250 ml (9 fl oz/1 cup) coconut milk.

Coffee

Reduce the vanilla to just 1 teaspoon and replace 80 ml (2½ fl oz/⅓ cup) of the milk with 80 ml (2½ fl oz/⅓ cup) freshly made espresso coffee. Replace half the caster sugar with brown sugar.

Lavender

Place 3 teaspoons edible lavender leaves in the milk when you first heat it. Set aside to infuse for 10 minutes, then strain out the lavender and gently reheat the milk before mixing into the eggs.

Sweetly spiced

Add your choice of spices to the pan when you first heat the milk. You can make it as mild or strong as you like; as a guide, try 1 cinnamon stick, a few fresh ginger slices, 2–3 cardamom pods, a good pinch of ground nutmeg and 2–3 cloves. When you take the milk off the heat, let it infuse for 10 minutes, then gently reheat and strain onto the egg mixture as you whisk.

This base is also perfect for the chai crème pâtissière below.

Tea or two

Place 2 tea bags of your choice (English breakfast, earl grey, houjicha, lapsang souchong, etc) in the milk mixture when you first heat it. When you take the milk off the heat, let it infuse for 10 minutes. Remove the tea bags, then gently reheat the milk again before mixing into the eggs.

If using matcha (powdered green tea), whisk 1½ tablespoons in with the egg mixture before you whisk in the hot milk.

For a **chai crème pâtissière**, use the Sweetly spiced crème pâtissière above as your base recipe, adding in 2 tea bags of black tea; you can also use coconut milk instead of dairy milk.

Amazing glaze
HOW SWEET THE SOUND...

If you'd like to glaze your doughnuts, omit the sugar-rolling step straight after cooking. Allow the doughnuts to cool completely before glazing. Dip one side of the cool doughnuts in the glaze, allow the excess to drip off, then place on a cake rack, glaze side up, until dry to the touch.

If you prefer a thicker layer of glaze, you can repeat the glazing process once the first layer of glaze has set. The caramel glaze is particularly luscious, and almost chewy when applied twice.

All the glazes here make enough for one single layer of glaze for 24 doughnuts, so make sure you double the quantity if double-dipping the whole batch.

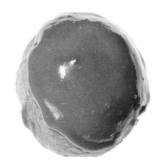

Lemon glaze

Mix 185 g (6½ oz/1½ cups) sifted icing sugar mixture with 3 tablespoons fresh, strained lemon juice and 2 drops of pure vanilla extract.

Cherry glaze

Mix 185 g (6½ oz/1½ cups) sifted icing sugar mixture with 3 tablespoons tart cherry juice (or half cherry juice, half cherry liqueur) and a few drops of pure vanilla extract.

Coffee glaze

Mix 185 g (6½ oz/1½ cups) sifted icing sugar mixture with 3 tablespoons espresso coffee (or half espresso, half milk) and a few drops of pure vanilla extract until smooth.

Rhubarb & rose glaze

Put 125 g (4½ oz/1 cup) chopped rhubarb in a saucepan, with 60 g (2¼ oz/½ cup) icing sugar mixture, 2 tablespoons water and 2 teaspoons butter. Stir to combine over medium heat. Allow the mixture to come to a rapid simmer, then bubble away for 5 minutes, or until the rhubarb is rather mushy. Push the juice into a bowl, through a fine sieve, by stirring briskly with a wooden spoon; discard the fibrous mass that collects in the sieve. Stir 165 g (5¾ oz/1⅓ cups) icing (confectioners') sugar and 1 teaspoon rosewater into the rhubarb purée and combine well.

Caramel glaze

Combine 185 g (6½ oz/1 cup) brown sugar, 1½ tablespoons unsalted butter and 2½ tablespoons cream in a saucepan. Stir over medium–high heat until the sugar has dissolved. Bring to the boil and cook, without stirring, for 5 minutes, or until it starts to smell like toffee. Whisk in ½ teaspoon pure vanilla extract and a pinch of fine sea salt. Remove from the heat and cool slightly, then glaze the doughnuts while the glaze is still fairly fluid.

For a **salted caramel glaze** simply increase the salt to ¼ teaspoon (or to your taste), and sprinkle a few salt flakes on top.

Red berry glaze (strawberry or raspberry)

Mix 185 g (6½ oz/1½ cups) icing sugar mixture with 3 tablespoons puréed strawberries or raspberries until smooth. Allow to sit for a few minutes, then stir well again.

Pineapple glaze

Mix 185 g (6½ oz/1½ cups) icing sugar mixture with ¼ teaspoon lemon juice and 3 tablespoons fresh (or tinned) strained, unsweetened pineapple juice.

Chocolate glaze

Sift 185 g (6½ oz/1½ cups) icing sugar mixture with 1½ tablespoons good unsweetened cocoa powder. Mix with 2 tablespoons plus 1 teaspoon water or milk, and a few drops of pure vanilla extract.

Vanilla glaze

Mix 185 g (6½ oz/1½ cups) sifted icing sugar mixture with 1 tablespoon plus 3 teaspoons water, and 1 teaspoon pure vanilla extract.

DOUGHNUT DESSERTS!

Have some fun with your doughnuts, fillings and glazes and turn them into inspired desserts with the works.

Here's a bunch of ideas to get you started. You'll find all the glazes on the previous page, and all the fillings on pages 60–61.

If you're using only one filling, you can simply pipe it into the doughnut; if using several fillings you can cut the doughnuts in half, fill them, then sandwich the bits back together.

Cappuccino

Cinnamon doughnut + Coffee crème pâtissière + Chocolate glaze drizzle.

Cherry on top

Plain doughnut + Cherry glaze + half Chocolate/half Coconut crème pâtissière.

Chocolate éclair

Plain doughnut + Chocolate glaze + Chocolate or Vanilla crème pâtissière + whipped cream.

Choc orange spice cake

Cinnamon doughnut + Chocolate crème pâtissière + orange marmalade + Chocolate glaze drizzle.

Chocolate caramel slice

Plain doughnut + Salted caramel glaze + Chocolate crème pâtissière.

Coffee éclair

Plain doughnut + Coffee glaze + Coffee crème pâtissière + whipped cream.

Cream bun

Cinnamon doughnut + Crème pâtissière + whipped cream + berry jam.

Crème brûlée

Plain doughnut + Caramel glaze + Vanilla crème pâtissière.

Finger bun

Plain doughnut + Strawberry glaze + Coconut crème pâtissière.

Lamington

Plain doughnut + Chocolate glaze + Coconut crème pâtissière + whipped cream.

Lemon cream dream

Cinnamon doughnut + Lemon fruit curd + whipped cream (optional).

Nana's nickers

Cinnamon doughnut + Lavender crème pâtissière.

Pine lime tropical dream

Plain doughnut + Pineapple glaze + Lime fruit curd + Coconut crème pâtissière.

Rose garden

Plain doughnut + Rhubarb & rose glaze + Vanilla crème pâtissière.

The Diana

Cinnamon doughnut + whipped cream cheese with lemon zest + sultanas (golden raisins) soaked in a little rum or black tea.

Tea & toast

Cinnamon doughnut + Tea or two crème pâtissière.

Trifle

Cinnamon doughnut + Vanilla crème pâtissière + strawberry jam mixed with a little sherry + whipped cream + toasted flaked almonds.

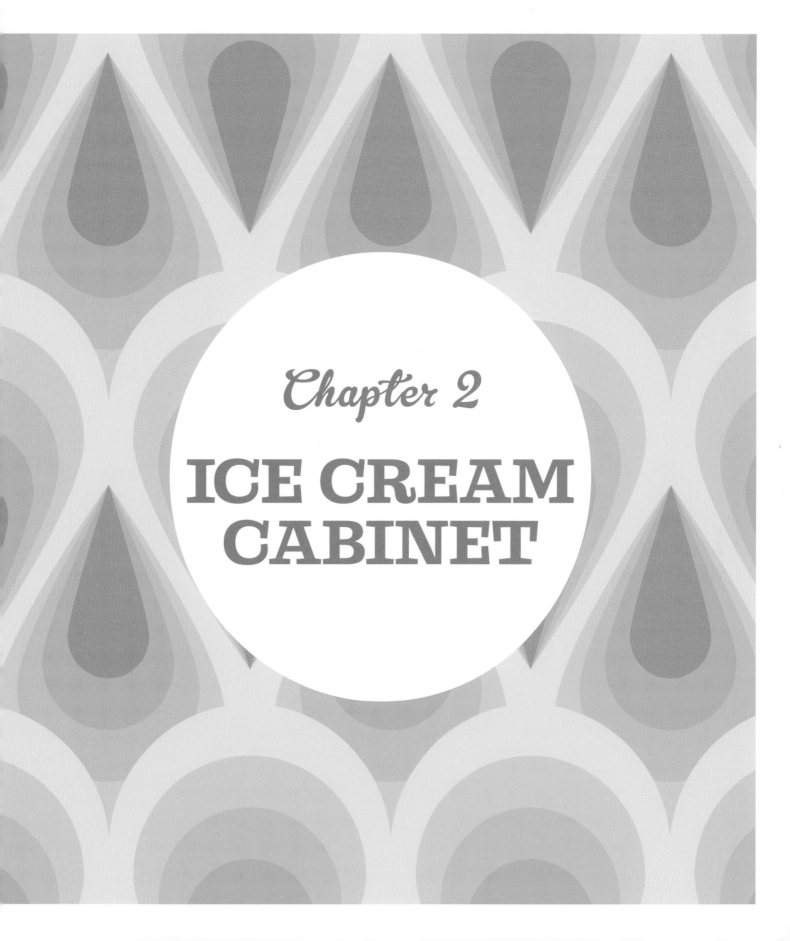

Chapter 2

ICE CREAM CABINET

AN INTEGRAL PART of every milkbar was the ice cream cabinet. When I was tall enough to stand on my tippy toes I'd peek through the glass into the deep, frosted metal cylinders containing alluring shades of icy goodness and try not to shake with excitement over which new flavour to try. I also found it hard not to imagine the milkbar attendants being vacuumed into the cabinet as they reached deep into the bottom of the canisters when the contents were low. Ice cream seemed all the more precious with the server's extra effort, and perceived risk, in extracting themselves from the freezer's jaws. In an added bonus, the same dangerous foraging was required for the milkshakes that would whiz and whirr in front of us. The music of milkbars.

Per capita, Australians are one of the world's biggest ice cream consumers. One might hazard a guess that it has something to do with our climate. Whether in a cone or cup, or on a stick, as long as it is icy, cold and sweet, we eat it by the bucketload. So it makes sense to me that we'd be better off eating ice cream made from pure, whole ingredients, and natural flavours and colours — rendering it almost a health food! Almost.

For ice cream connoisseurs who are inspired to regularly make their own concoctions, I'd recommend investing in a quality ice cream maker, which will produce a much smoother texture than could ever be achieved by hand churning. The top of the line models freeze as they churn, forming very fine ice crystals and velvety results — although you'll need deep pockets to buy one of these.

Home-made ice cream is the best ice cream. It's more dense and creamy than most commercial brands, but do note that because it doesn't have preservatives, it won't last as long... but that's probably not going to be a problem.

True blue vanilla ice cream

There is something so pure and decadent about this most divine vanilla ice cream. I'm mighty fussy and don't enjoy most store-bought vanilla ice cream, but it is probably a good thing it doesn't taste this good. This is the real deal. Try making it just once and you'll be hooked!

Makes 1 litre (35 fl oz)

1 vanilla bean

500 ml (17 fl oz/2 cups) thin (pouring) cream

325 ml (11 fl oz) full-cream milk

9 egg yolks

165 g (5¾ oz/¾ cup) caster (superfine) sugar

Using a small sharp knife, split the vanilla bean down its length, scrape out the seeds, then place both the pod and seeds in a saucepan. Add the cream and milk. Bring almost to the boil over medium–high heat, then remove from the heat and leave to infuse for 20 minutes.

In a bowl, whisk together the egg yolks and sugar. Whisking constantly, gradually pour in the infused milk mixture. Pour into a clean saucepan and stir over medium–low heat for 15 minutes, or until the mixture has thickened to a thin custard consistency and easily coats the back of a spoon. Cool slightly, then pour into a bowl. Cover and chill for 2 hours, or until cold.

Strain, then churn and freeze in an ice cream machine according to the manufacturer's instructions. (Alternatively, you can pour the custard mixture into a large shallow cake tin and freeze for 2–3 hours, or until just frozen around the edges. Whisk to evenly distribute the ice crystals through the mixture. Repeat this every hour until the mixture is frozen and evenly textured.)

Transfer to a 1 litre (35 fl oz/4 cup) plastic container. Smooth the surface over, top with a sheet of baking paper, then pop the lid on. The ice cream will keep in the freezer for up to 1 week, but tastes best if eaten within a few days.

VANILLI MANILLI

No imposters here, simply riffs on vanilla...

Ginger ice cream

Use only ½ vanilla bean, and add 1½ tablespoons ground ginger or 100 g (3½ oz) finely chopped fresh ginger to infuse the milk in the first step; strain the fresh ginger out before churning. For **honey ginger ice cream**, substitute honey for half the sugar.

Coco-berry crunch

Just as the ice cream is firming up, stir in some desiccated coconut, Strawberry syrup (page 218) and biscuit (cookie) pieces. Before you seal and freeze the ice cream, sprinkle the top with extra strawberry syrup and desiccated coconut.

Cappuccino swirl

When the ice cream is almost frozen, add a drizzle of Coffee syrup (page 218) and some finely grated chocolate and churn until it just mixes through. Drizzle the top with coffee syrup before sealing and freezing.

Muesli & milk

Stir a small amount of honey-toasted oats, toasted chopped nuts and toasted shredded coconut through the ice cream just before it firms up.

Rhubarb crumble

As the ice cream starts to firm, stir in some poached rhubarb, toasted oats, biscuit (cookie) pieces, toasted shredded coconut, ground cinnamon and chopped toasted pecans. (Instead of rhubarb, use poached or tinned pears, peaches, apricots or apple for different ice cream crumbles.)

Lemon ice cream

This luscious lovely tastes like creamy frozen lemon curd. It makes me want to revert to a childhood I never had, skipping through fields in a pale lemon frock, plucking tiny daisies for threading into a crown of flowers. For someone who only ever wears black and was dressed in navy and brown corduroy as a kid, that is quite the wishful-thinking stretch.

Makes 1 litre (35 fl oz)

½ vanilla bean

325 ml (11 fl oz) thin (pouring) cream

325 ml (11 fl oz) full-cream milk

1 tablespoon finely grated lemon zest

8 egg yolks

220 g (7¾ oz/1 cup) caster (superfine) sugar

125 ml (4 fl oz/½ cup) strained, fresh lemon juice, plus an extra 2–4 teaspoons for finishing

Lemony lickits

Lemon delicious
As the ice cream is firming up, stir some toasted shredded coconut through.

Lemon tart
Just as the ice cream is firming up, stir in some broken-up pieces of well-cooked Sweet shortcrust pastry (page 224).

Lemon nutter
Stir some chopped toasted macadamia nuts or Vienna almonds (page 138) through the ice cream as it starts to firm up.

Put the vanilla bean, cream, milk and lemon zest in a saucepan. Bring almost to the boil over medium–high heat, then remove from the heat and leave to infuse for 20 minutes.

In a bowl, whisk together the egg yolks and sugar until pale and creamy. Gradually pour in the infused milk mixture, whisking constantly. Stir in the lemon juice.

Pour into a clean saucepan and stir over medium–low heat for 15 minutes, or until the mixture has thickened to a thin custard consistency and coats the back of a spoon. Remove from the heat, cool slightly, then pour into a bowl. Cover and chill for 2 hours, or until cold. Stir in a little extra lemon juice to suit your taste.

Strain, then churn and freeze in an ice cream machine according to the manufacturer's instructions. (Alternatively, you can pour the custard mixture into a large shallow cake tin and freeze for 2–3 hours, or until just frozen around the edges. Whisk to evenly distribute the ice crystals through the mixture. Repeat this every hour until the mixture is frozen and evenly textured.)

Transfer to a 1 litre (35 fl oz/4 cup) plastic container. Smooth the surface over, top with a sheet of baking paper, then pop the lid on. The ice cream will keep in the freezer for up to 1 week, but tastes best if eaten within a few days.

Strawberry ice cream

One summer when I was very young we went strawberry picking as a family. I'm pretty sure we ate more than what went into the punnet we paid for, and I don't think that was a surprise to the farm owners. On the car ride there my father asked me if I wanted manure or cream on my strawberries. After thinking about it I went for the manure — I didn't know what it was but I thought it sounded exotic. Always the gourmand... Ask me again and I'll take the strawberries and cream — in fact I'll take 'em together in this gorgeous pink ice cream, or one of the variations on the opposite page.

Makes 1 litre (35 fl oz)

½ vanilla bean

310 ml (10¾ fl oz/1¼ cups) thin (pouring) cream

310 ml (10¾ fl oz/1¼ cups) full-cream milk

8 egg yolks

165 g (5¾ oz/¾ cup) caster (superfine) sugar

170 ml (5½ fl oz/⅔ cup) strained strawberry purée, made from ripe, fragrant fresh strawberries

1 tablespoon strawberry liqueur (optional)

Put the vanilla bean, cream and milk in a saucepan. Bring almost to the boil over medium–high heat, then remove from the heat and leave to infuse for 20 minutes.

In a bowl, whisk the egg yolks and sugar. Gradually pour in the infused milk mixture, whisking constantly.

Pour into a clean saucepan and stir over medium–low heat for 15 minutes, or until the mixture has thickened to a thin custard consistency and coats the back of a spoon. Remove from the heat, cool slightly, then pour into a bowl. Cover and chill for 2 hours, or until cold.

Strain, then stir the strawberry purée and liqueur through. Churn and freeze in an ice cream machine according to the manufacturer's instructions. (Alternatively, you can pour the custard mixture into a large shallow cake tin and freeze for 2–3 hours, or until just frozen around the edges. Whisk to evenly distribute the ice crystals through the mixture. Repeat this every hour until the mixture is frozen and evenly textured.)

Transfer to a 1 litre (35 fl oz/4 cup) plastic container. Smooth the surface over, top with a sheet of baking paper, then pop the lid on. The ice cream will keep in the freezer for up to 1 week, but tastes best if eaten within a few days.

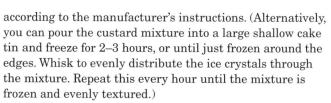

Strawberry ripple

Swirl Strawberry syrup (page 218) through the ice cream as it firms up.

Strawberry white chocolate crunch

As the ice cream is firming up, stir in some grated white chocolate and crushed speculoos biscuits (spiced, caramelised Belgian cookies).

Strawberry coconut ice

Line a small loaf (bar) tin with plastic wrap, spray with cooking oil spray and sprinkle liberally with desiccated coconut. When the strawberry ice cream comes out of the ice cream machine, scoop enough into the tin to form a layer 3 cm (1¼ inches) deep; spread over gently with a spatula to ensure it is even. Freeze for 1 hour. Top with a layer of Coconut ice cream (page 99) and freeze until ready to serve. Dip briefly in hot water, then invert onto a serving plate. Garnish with strawberries and, if you want to be extra decadent, drizzle with condensed milk.

Golden caramel ice cream

I like to add some lemon zest to this recipe, as it cuts the sweetness of the caramel, but feel free to leave it out for a more pure caramel flavour.

Makes 1 litre (35 fl oz)

150 g (5½ oz/⅔ cup) caster (superfine) sugar

375 ml (13 fl oz/1½ cups) thin (pouring) cream

500 ml (17 fl oz/2 cups) full-cream milk

½ vanilla bean

a 5 cm (2 inch) strip of lemon zest, no white pith (optional)

8 egg yolks

Put the sugar and 2 tablespoons water into a saucepan. Stir over high heat, just until the sugar has dissolved. Stop stirring and cook for 3–4 minutes, swirling the pan occasionally to encourage even caramelisation, until the caramel is dark golden and smells of toffee.

Remove the pan from the heat. Using a long-handled metal spoon, stir in the cream — be careful as it will splutter and the caramel may seize. Place back over medium heat and stir occasionally for about 1 minute, or until the caramel and cream flow freely.

Meanwhile, put the milk, vanilla bean and lemon zest in a saucepan over medium–high heat. Bring almost to the boil, then remove from the heat and set aside for 5 minutes, or until your caramel mixture is ready.

When the caramel is ready, pour the hot milk into the pan and whisk with the caramel. Cool slightly.

Whisk the egg yolks in a bowl. Gradually mix in the milk and caramel mixture. Pour into a clean saucepan and cook over medium–low heat, stirring regularly, for 12 minutes, or until the mixture thickens to a thin custard consistency and coats the back of a spoon.

Remove from the heat, cool slightly, then pour into a bowl. Cover and chill for 2 hours, or until cold.

Strain, then churn and freeze in an ice cream machine according to the manufacturer's instructions. (Alternatively, you can pour the custard mixture into a large shallow cake tin and freeze for 2–3 hours, or until just frozen around the edges. Whisk to evenly distribute the ice crystals through the mixture. Repeat this every hour until the mixture is frozen and evenly textured.)

Transfer to a 1 litre (35 fl oz/4 cup) plastic container. Smooth the surface over, top with a sheet of baking paper, then pop the lid on. The ice cream will keep in the freezer for up to 1 week, but tastes best if eaten within a few days.

Caramel capers

Salted caramel

In the last stages of churning, add 2 teaspoons sea salt flakes, or to taste.

Caramel nut

In the last stages of churning, add ½ cup chopped toasted nuts of your choice — pecan, walnut or peanut are my favourites for this, but Brazil nuts, cashews, macadamias and almonds would all work very well too.

Caramel ripple

As you are transferring scoops of the caramel ice cream to a storage container, drizzle with Caramel syrup (page 217) between scoops. Smooth the top down when you are done and drizzle a little more caramel syrup over the top.

Baklava

In the final stages of churning, add a small handful of chopped, toasted pistachio nuts and walnuts, a teaspoon of ground cinnamon, a small pinch of ground cloves, and a small handful of filo pastry that has been buttered and baked until golden, then broken into small pieces. When serving, drizzle the top with honey mixed with orange blossom water.

Dairy milk chocolate ice cream

This rich, smooth-as-silk chocolate indulgence is sure to become a household staple. Sorry.

Makes 1 litre (35 fl oz)

300 ml (10½ fl oz) thin (pouring) cream

400 ml (14 fl oz) full-cream milk

8 egg yolks

60 g (2¼ oz/⅓ cup) brown sugar

75 g (2¾ oz/⅓ cup) caster (superfine) sugar

1½ teaspoons good-quality unsweetened cocoa powder

½–1 teaspoon pure vanilla extract

200 g (7 oz) good-quality milk chocolate, chopped

Put the cream and milk in a saucepan. Bring almost to the boil over medium–high heat, then remove from the heat.

In a bowl, whisk together the egg yolks, brown and caster sugar, cocoa powder and vanilla until well combined. Gradually pour in the hot milk mixture, whisking constantly until smooth.

Pour into a clean saucepan and stir over medium–low heat for 12–15 minutes, or until the mixture has thickened to a thin custard consistency and coats the back of a spoon. Remove from the heat, then add the chocolate and stir until it has melted and the custard is an even colour. Cool slightly, then strain into a bowl. Cover and chill for 2 hours, or until cold.

Set up an ice cream machine and churn and freeze the mixture according to the manufacturer's instructions. (Alternatively, you can pour the custard mixture into a large shallow cake tin and freeze for 2–3 hours, or until just frozen around the edges. Whisk to evenly distribute the ice crystals through the mixture. Repeat this every hour until the mixture is frozen and evenly textured.)

Transfer to a 1 litre (35 fl oz/4 cup) plastic container. Smooth the surface over, top with a sheet of baking paper, then pop the lid on. The ice cream will keep in the freezer for up to 1 week, but tastes best if eaten within a few days.

CHOC MY WORLD!

Milky white

Use good-quality white chocolate instead of dark, and use only caster sugar.

Dark side of the moon

Use dark chocolate instead of milk chocolate, and use only brown sugar.

Milk chocolate choc-chip

Add a handful of chocolate chips or finely chopped chocolate to the ice cream just before the final stages of churning, while the ice cream is still soft enough to mix them through.

Choc mint chip

Add a handful of scrunched fresh mint leaves into the initial milk mixture and allow to infuse with the vanilla. Add some dark chocolate chips or finely chopped dark chocolate in the final stages of churning.

Choc à l'orange

Infuse 3 teaspoons orange zest in the custard base and use dark chocolate.

Choc malted

Once the chocolate has melted, stir 2–3 tablespoons malt powder into the custard and whisk until completely dissolved.

Rocky road

Just as the ice cream is firming up, stir in chopped Marshmallow (page 117), nuts, glacé cherries and toasted shredded coconut.

Scorched almond

Stir Chocolate syrup (page 217) and toasted almonds through the ice cream just as it is firming up.

Chocolate ginger

Stir chopped Crystallised ginger (page 141) through the ice cream just as it is firming up.

Liquorice ice cream

Our house was always stocked with liquorice straps, twists, sticks and allsorts. Although mum regularly devoured chocolate bullets when I was in the womb, I've only recently become a fan of the flavour. Who knew liquorice ice cream would totally float my boat?

Makes 1 litre (35 fl oz)

150 g (5½ oz/1¼ cups) finely chopped liquorice, either store-bought or home-made (page 131); store-bought will give a deeper colour

500 ml (17 fl oz/2 cups) full-cream milk

310 ml (10¾ fl oz/1¼ cups) thin (pouring) cream

¼ teaspoon pure vanilla extract

8 egg yolks

75 g (2¾ oz/⅓ cup) caster (superfine) sugar

a pinch of sea salt

Check these out!

Liquorice allsorts

In a loaf (bar) tin, add a layer of Liquorice ice cream, then a layer of Strawberry ice cream (page 74), and finally a layer of Lemon ice cream (page 73) — leaving 1 hour between each layer for them to set. Slice to serve.

Chocolate bullet bar

Half-fill a loaf (bar) tin with Chocolate ice cream (page 78), smooth over, then freeze for 1 hour. Fill to the top with Liquorice ice cream, smooth over, then cover and freeze for 3–4 hours before releasing from the mould. Drizzle melted dark chocolate over, allow it to set, then cut into slices to serve.

Put the liquorice, milk, cream and vanilla in a saucepan. Stir regularly over medium–high heat until the liquorice has melted; there may still be a few lumps left. Bring almost to the boil, then remove from the heat and allow to infuse for 10 minutes.

In a bowl, whisk together the egg yolks sugar and sea salt until thick and creamy. Gradually pour in the infused milk mixture, whisking constantly.

Pour into a clean saucepan and stir over medium–low heat for about 15 minutes, or until the mixture has thickened to a thin custard consistency and coats the back of a spoon. Remove from the heat, cool slightly, then pour into a bowl. Cover and chill for 2–3 hours, or until cold.

Strain, then churn and freeze in an ice cream machine according to the manufacturer's instructions. (Alternatively you can pour the custard mixture into a large shallow cake tin and freeze for 2–3 hours, or until just frozen around the edges. Whisk to evenly distribute the ice crystals through the mixture. Repeat this every hour until the mixture is frozen and evenly textured.)

Transfer to a 1 litre (35 fl oz/4 cup) plastic container. Smooth the surface over, top with a sheet of baking paper, then pop the lid on. The ice cream will keep in the freezer for up to 1 week, but tastes best if eaten within a few days.

Coffee ice cream

Australians love their coffee almost as much as their ice cream. While tiramisu was the only coffee-flavoured wonder doing the rounds when I was growing up, these days coffee gelato, frappés and affogatos all rank highly on the summer hit list. This recipe makes a great base for drinks, but is also perfect just on its own... or drizzled with some Coffee syrup (page 218) or Chocolate syrup (page 217). Caffeine, dairy, sugar, icy... what's not to love?

Makes 1 litre (35 fl oz)

½ vanilla bean

300 ml (10½ fl oz) thin (pouring) cream

250 ml (9 fl/oz/1 cup) full-cream milk

180 ml (6 fl oz/¾ cup) freshly made espresso coffee

8 egg yolks

45 g (1½ oz/¼ cup) brown sugar

75 g (2¾ oz/⅓ cup) caster (superfine) sugar

Put the vanilla bean, cream and milk in a saucepan. Bring almost to the boil over medium–high heat, then remove from the heat. Add the coffee and leave to infuse for 20 minutes.

In a bowl, whisk together the egg yolks and all the sugar. Gradually pour in the infused milk mixture, whisking constantly.

Pour the mixture into a clean saucepan and stir over medium–low heat for about 15 minutes, or until the mixture has thickened to a thin custard consistency and coats the back of a spoon. Remove from the heat, cool slightly, then pour into a bowl. Cover and chill for 2 hours, or until cold.

Strain, then churn and freeze in an ice cream machine according to the manufacturer's instructions. (Alternatively, you can pour the custard mixture into a large shallow cake tin and freeze for 2–3 hours, or until just frozen around the edges. Whisk to evenly distribute the ice crystals through the mixture. Repeat this every hour until the mixture is frozen and evenly textured.)

Transfer to a 1 litre (35 fl oz/4 cup) plastic container. Smooth the surface over, top with a sheet of baking paper, then pop the lid on. The ice cream will keep in the freezer for up to 1 week, but tastes best if eaten within a few days.

COFFEE-A-GO-GO

Coffee almond

Stir toasted slivered almonds or chopped Vienna almonds (page 138) through the ice cream as it firms up.

Coffee nut brittle

Stir about 4 tablespoons of chopped Nut brittle (page 110) through the ice cream as it firms up.

Coffee caramel swirl

As you are transferring scoops of the coffee ice cream to a storage container, drizzle with Caramel syrup (page 217) between scoops. Smooth the top down when you are done and drizzle a little more Caramel syrup over the top.

Coffee maple walnut

As the ice cream firms up, stir in some toasted chopped walnuts, then swirl some maple syrup through.

Mocha

Add 100 g (3½ oz) grated dark chocolate to the hot custard mixture just after it has thickened; whisk until melted and evenly coloured.

Rum & raisin ice cream

My mum isn't a drinker by any stretch of the imagination, but she did in the past enjoy a fine rum and raisin ice cream. For years, she lost interest in ice cream altogether (I must have got the 'frosty treat–abuser gene' from my dad). However, she's recently rediscovered it, and not a minute too soon, giving my home-made rum and raisin the big thumbs up. Covering mum's ears for a minute, there is something very sexy about this grownups-only iced dessert.

Makes 1 litre (35 fl oz)

60 g (2¼ oz/⅓ cup) raisins

60 ml (2 fl oz/¼ cup) good-quality dark rum

500 ml (17 fl oz/2 cups) full-cream milk

375 ml (13 fl oz/1½ cups) cream

½ vanilla bean

8 egg yolks

60 g (2¼ oz/⅓ cup) brown sugar

110 g (3¾ oz/½ cup) caster (superfine) sugar

Put the raisins and rum in a small non-metallic bowl. Cover and leave to soak overnight.

Put the milk, cream and vanilla bean in a saucepan. Bring almost to the boil over medium–high heat, then remove from the heat and leave to infuse for 10 minutes.

In a bowl, whisk together the egg yolks and all the sugar until thick and creamy. Gradually pour in the infused milk mixture, whisking constantly.

Pour into a clean saucepan and stir over medium–low heat for about 15 minutes, or until the mixture has thickened to a thin custard consistency and coats the back of a spoon. Remove from the heat, cool slightly, then pour into a bowl. Cover and chill for 2–3 hours, or until cold.

Strain, then churn and freeze in an ice cream machine according to the manufacturer's instructions, but adding in the raisins (and any leftover rum if you like — I say the more the merrier!) just as the ice cream is firming up. The alcohol may break down the ice cream slightly, but it will freeze up again — although it will be a little softer than most of the ice creams in this book. But you won't care. It is that good. (Alternatively you can pour the custard mixture into a large shallow cake tin and freeze for 2–3 hours, or until just frozen around the edges. Whisk to evenly distribute the ice crystals through the mixture. Repeat this every hour until the mixture is frozen and evenly textured, folding the raisins through after the final whisking.)

Transfer to a 1 litre (35 fl oz/4 cup) plastic container. Smooth the surface over, top with a sheet of baking paper, then pop the lid on. The ice cream will keep in the freezer for up to 1 week, but tastes best if eaten within a few days.

Dark & stormy

Stir finely chopped pieces of glacé ginger into the ice cream as it starts to firm up.

Choc rum raisin

Add the rum-soaked raisins to the Chocolate ice cream (page 78).

Caramel rum raisin

Add the rum-soaked raisins to Golden caramel ice cream (page 76).

Hazelnut rum raisin

Add a half quantity of rum-soaked raisins and a handful of toasted chopped hazelnuts to the Caramel hazelnut ice cream (page 96) base, then store the ice cream in the container for scooping, as it will be too soft for turning into ice blocks.

Ice cream cones

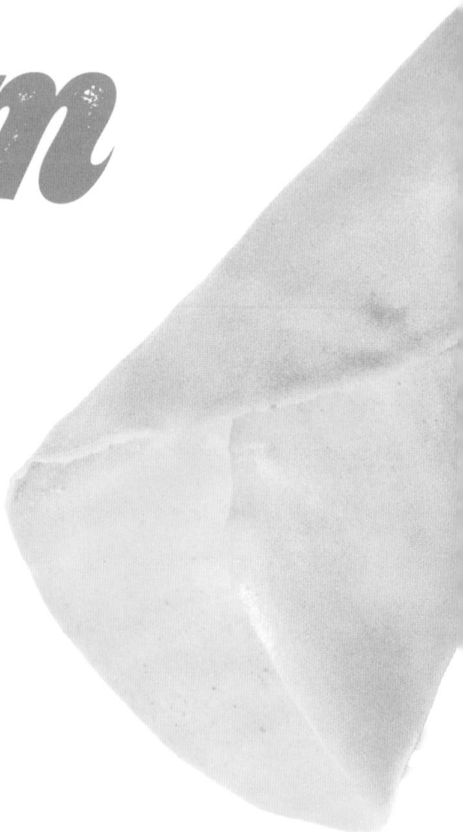

If you are going to make your own ice cream, why not try your own cones too? They are reasonably simple to make, and if they don't look quite as pretty as the commercial brands, they will make up for it in flavour.

Makes 12 cones

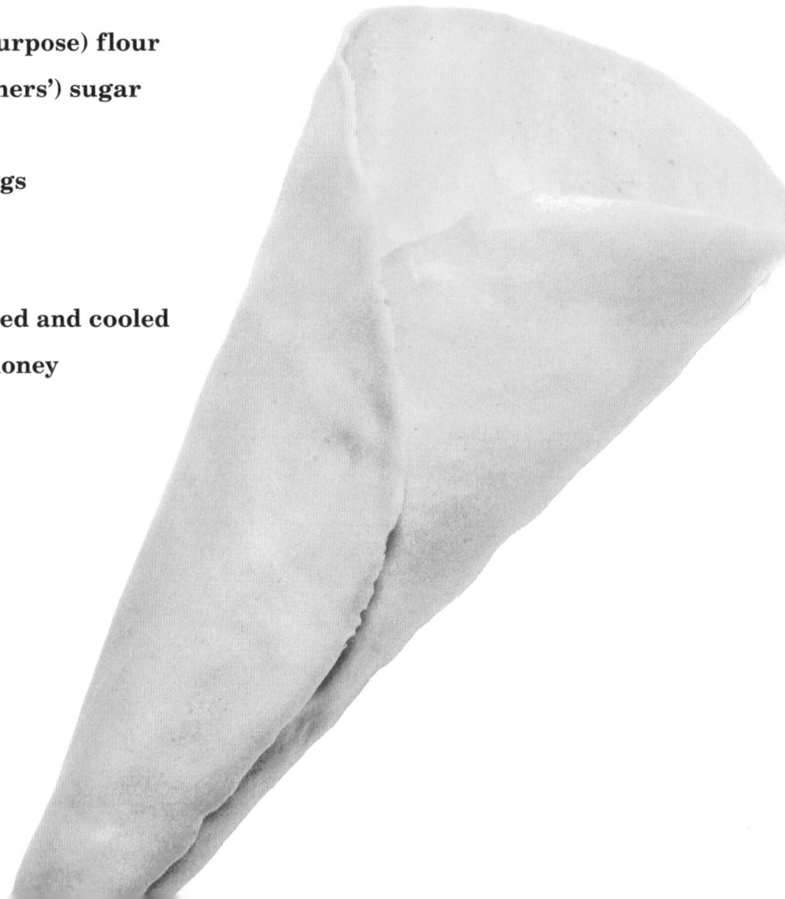

185 g (6½ oz/1¼ cups) plain (all-purpose) flour

85 g (3 oz/⅔ cup) icing (confectioners') sugar

a pinch of sea salt

3 egg whites, from 65 g (2½ oz) eggs

½ teaspoon pure vanilla extract

2 tablespoons milk

65 g (2½ oz) unsalted butter, melted and cooled

1½ tablespoons golden syrup or honey

Sift the flour, icing sugar and salt into a bowl and make a well in the centre. In a jug, combine the egg whites, vanilla, milk, melted butter and golden syrup, then pour into the well, using a balloon whisk to mix the batter until smooth and lump free. It should be the consistency of a thick pancake batter. Cover and refrigerate for at least 2 hours, or up to 3 days, before using.

Ideally, you'll have an ice cream cone mould from a kitchenware shop — or if you're handy, you can form a cone shape by compacting scrunched-up foil into a cone shape, making sure the wide end is at least 6 cm (2½ inches) in diameter, and wrap the outside with a layer of baking paper, so the biscuit cone will remove more easily. You'll also need a folded tea towel to help you cope with the heat of the cone — the batter needs to be shaped while still piping hot.

When ready to cook the batter, preheat the oven to 150°C (300°F). Lightly spray two baking trays with cooking oil spray. On each of two sheets of baking paper large enough to fit the trays, draw a 16 cm (6¼ inch) diameter circle with pencil. Place the baking paper, pencil side down, onto each tray, smoothing them over to help them adhere and keep them sturdy.

Drop 2 tablespoons of the batter into the centre of each circle, then use a small off-set spatula to spread the mixture evenly to fill the circles — they should be an even 2 mm (1/16 inch) thickness all over.

Place one tray in the oven and cook for 14–15 minutes, or until golden all over. Add the second tray to the oven about 5 minutes after the first, and cook as before. You stagger the cooking of the cones, so you have time to mould them while they're still hot. (If the phone interrupts you and a 'cone' sets flat before you have a chance to roll it, simply pop it back in the oven briefly to soften.) When the first tray is ready, remove it from the oven. Slip a spatula underneath one of the rounds. Wearing clean rubber gloves, or using a folded-over tea towel to protect you from the heat, quickly wrap the round of batter around the mould, at the same time pinching the pointed end to seal it closed — you will need both hands for this. Hold around the wider cone and the tip for a minute or two, until the shape holds, then allow the cone to cool on the mould before removing to a tray. By this stage your next cone should be ready for rolling, so repeat as before.

If your cone tip doesn't seal too well, wrap some baking paper around the tip, or pop a little piece of marshmallow into the cone before filling with ice cream; this will help stop the drips.

Repeat the spreading, cooking and rolling methods until you have used up all the batter. You should end up with about 12 cones (or bowls; see note below).

When cooled, fill with scoops of your favourite ice cream and enjoy.

The cones are best eaten the same day, but will last for up to 1 week in an airtight container. If you don't use your cones straight away, they may soften a little. Give them a quick blast in a hot oven; when they cool down they will crisp up again.

NOTE *If you have acquired 'asbestos' hands from working in a professional kitchen, you can try rolling freehand. Put a folded tea towel on your left hand (if you are right-handed, and vice versa if not). Place the cooked round on top, then make a claw with that hand so the round starts to curl over into a loose cone shape, using your free hand to help it into a neater cone, squeezing the tip of the cone to seal. Hold for a minute or so, using the tea towel as a buffer from the heat. You can also just pop the round over a small upturned bowl or ramekin, using the tea towel to help shape it — you'll end up with your own little ice cream dish when set.*

Cone creative

You may need to channel your own inner child for more whacky ways to flavour or decorate your cones — but here's a selection destined to become new favourites.

Hundreds & thousands

Lightly sprinkle around the edges of the batter rounds with hundreds and thousands or sprinkles before baking.

Coconut cones

Lightly sprinkle around the edges of the batter rounds with desiccated coconut before baking.

Choc-dipped

Dip the open end of the cone into melted good-quality chocolate of your choice; leave to set on a tray lined with baking paper.

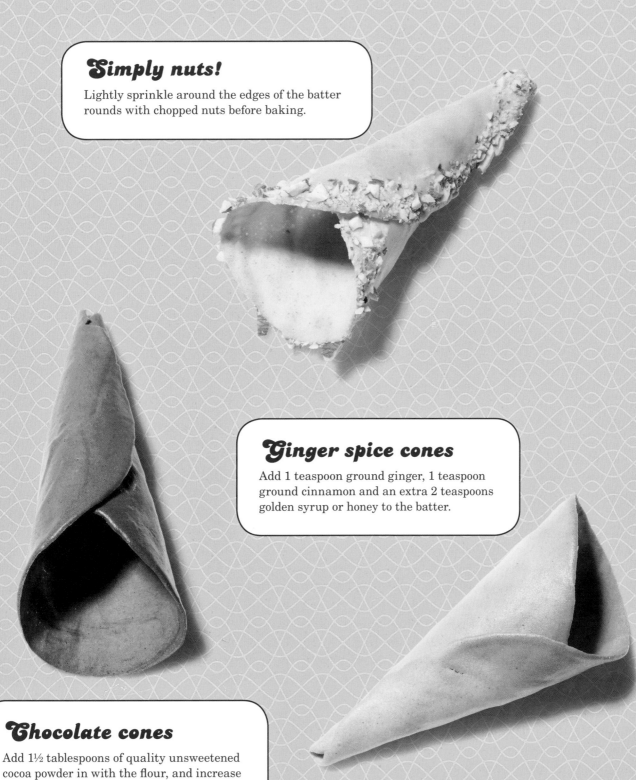

Simply nuts!

Lightly sprinkle around the edges of the batter rounds with chopped nuts before baking.

Ginger spice cones

Add 1 teaspoon ground ginger, 1 teaspoon ground cinnamon and an extra 2 teaspoons golden syrup or honey to the batter.

Chocolate cones

Add 1½ tablespoons of quality unsweetened cocoa powder in with the flour, and increase the golden syrup or honey by 1 tablespoon.

Two things
come to mind when I'm
reminiscing about ice cream
sundaes and banana splits. Firstly,
'The Drugstore', a 1950s-style diner in
Sydney's Double Bay that we'd frequent
on weekends when I was a kid; as a family
we'd trek across for the best hot fudge
sundaes and banana splits in town,
served by roller-skating waitresses.
Secondly, early-weekend mornings,
when *The Banana Splits* show
aired on the telly!

Banana splits

If you're old enough to remember the infectious tunes and goofy antics of the aforementioned Hanna-Barbera TV show, you'll perhaps appreciate a good old-fashioned banana split too! Watching *The Banana Splits* while eating an actual banana split was pretty potent for a pre-teen; watching re-runs online immediately sends me back to carefree weekends of fun and frivolity. What the heck happened to those? *Tra la laa la la-la laaaaaaaaaah... One banana, two banana, three banana, four...*

Simply cut a banana in half lengthways, place in a long serving dish and add your choice of toppings below.

Serves 1

Bananarama
Rum & raisin ice cream (page 84)

Caramel syrup (page 217)

whipped cream

toasted shredded coconut

Banana cream pie
Lemon ice cream (page 73)

Crème pâtissière (page 61)

whipped cream

chopped Vienna almonds (page 138)

Banana coffee haze
Caramel hazelnut ice cream (page 96)

Coffee syrup (page 218)

whipped cream

chopped toasted hazelnuts

Banana bender
Mango ice cream (page 99)

Coconut ice cream (page 99)

Passionfruit syrup (page 219)

whipped cream

toasted crushed macadamia nuts

Old fashioned
Vanilla ice cream (page 71)

Chocolate syrup (page 217)

toasted crushed peanuts or almonds

whipped cream

maraschino cherry with a stem

Sundae fundae

Simply layer the ingredients in a tall, wide sundae glass.

Neapolitan

Vanilla ice cream (page 71)

Strawberry ice cream (page 74)

Chocolate ice cream (page 78)

Chocolate syrup (page 217)

fresh sliced strawberries

whipped cream

Hazelnut choc top

Chocolate ice cream (page 78)

Caramel hazelnut ice cream (page 96)

Chocolate syrup (page 217)

whipped cream

toasted chopped hazelnuts

Lemon meringue pie

Coconut ice cream (page 99)

Vanilla ice cream (page 71)

Lemon fruit curd (page 60)

broken meringue

whipped cream

crumbled biscuits (cookies)

Liquorice sherbet

Liquorice ice cream (page 81)

Lemon ice cream (page 73)

Strawberry ice cream (page 74)

Strawberry syrup (page 218)

whipped cream

finely slivered liquorice straps

Fizzy sherbet powder (page 115)

Anzac cookie

Vanilla ice cream (page 71)

Lemon ice cream (page 73)

toasted oats

toasted shredded coconut

toasted macadamia nuts

toasted almonds

whipped cream

golden syrup or honey

Caramel &
HAZELNUT
HAPPY STICKS

Destined to put a smile on your dial, this combination of smooth hazelnut ice cream cloaked in milk chocolate and rolled in crushed caramelised spice cookies adds up to one dreamy dessert-on-a-stick!

Makes 6

125 g (4½ oz) speculoos biscuits (spiced, caramelised Belgian cookies)

400 g (14 oz) good-quality milk chocolate, finely chopped; you can use white chocolate too

50 g (1¾ oz) Copha (white vegetable shortening) or solid coconut oil

Caramel hazelnut ice cream

110 g (3¾ oz/½ cup) caster (superfine) sugar

250 ml (9 fl oz/1 cup) thin (pouring) cream

310 ml (10¾ fl oz/1¼ cups) full-cream milk

75 g (2¾ oz/½ cup) hazelnuts, well toasted, then ground

1 tablespoon malt powder

4 egg yolks

½ teaspoon pure vanilla extract

To make the ice cream, put the sugar in a heavy-based saucepan over medium–high heat. When it starts to dissolve and caramelise, start swirling the pan regularly until the sugar is a dark, honey-toned, even caramel, then immediately pour in the cream — be careful as it will spit and splutter. Use a long-handled whisk to mix the caramel and cream together over the heat — the cold cream will set the caramel at first, but eventually it will melt back to liquid form. When this happens, add the milk and bring to a simmer. Add the ground hazelnuts and the malt powder and cook for a further 5 minutes, then remove from the heat and allow to infuse for 20 minutes.

Whisk the egg yolks and vanilla in a bowl. Gently reheat the milk mixture over medium heat; when it comes to a simmer, remove from the heat and cool very slightly. Strain through a fine sieve, then whisk into your egg yolk mixture.

Pour the mixture into a clean saucepan and stir over medium–low heat for 8–10 minutes, or until the mixture thickens and coats the back of a spoon. Do not allow to boil. Remove from the heat, strain into a bowl and allow to cool. Cover and refrigerate until cold.

Set up an ice cream machine and freeze the mixture according to manufacturer's instructions. (Alternatively, you can pour the custard mixture into a large shallow cake tin and freeze for 2–3 hours, or until just frozen around the edges. Whisk to evenly distribute the ice crystals through the mixture. Repeat this every hour until the mixture is frozen and evenly textured.)

Spoon the ice cream mixture into six 90 ml (3 fl oz) ice cream moulds. Pop on the lids with the sticks that come with the moulds, then freeze overnight.

Put the biscuits in a food processor. Using the pulse button, process until you have 2–3 mm ($\frac{1}{16}$–$\frac{1}{8}$ inch) crumbs. (Alternatively, pop the biscuits in a snaplock bag and tap them with a rolling pin until crumbs are formed.) Store in an airtight container until ready to coat the ice creams.

When the ice creams are frozen, tip half the biscuit crumbs onto a plate.

Melt the chocolate and Copha together in a saucepan over low heat, stirring occasionally with a metal spoon, until the mixture is smooth and liquid. Pour into a small container, just a little wider than the ice creams, but around 15 cm (6 inches) deep — the chocolate mixture needs to be deeper than the ice creams; a milkshake container could be ideal. Allow the chocolate mixture to cool to room temperature, but do not allow to set; if it does, you'll need to gently melt it again.

Working quickly, and one at a time, hold an ice cream by the stick and dip it into the chocolate, so the chocolate completely covers the ice cream. Immediately withdraw it, briefly allowing any excess chocolate to drop off. Pat both sides into the biscuit crumbs, adding the remaining biscuit crumbs to the plate when the first half gets low, or too stuck together to evenly coat the chocolate. Place the ice cream in the freezer, on a tray lined with baking paper.

Repeat with all the ice creams, stacking them on top of each other, but separated by sheets of baking paper, and storing them in an airtight container. Refrigerate overnight again before serving. Use within 1 week.

Mango coconut ice bars

These were inspired by the real-fruit ice cream bars my dad used to bring home from the milkbar, wrapped in newspaper to keep them cool. An Australian creation, these bars became an immediate hit when they were first introduced back in 1957, for being so very refreshing and tasting of real fruit — as they still do almost 60 years later. Some things don't change, thankfully.

*Makes 30 bars, about
10 cm (4 inches) long*

50 g (1¾ oz/⅔ cup) lightly toasted
  shredded coconut, or 90 g (3¼ oz/⅔ cup)
  finely chopped toasted macadamia nuts
  (optional)

Mango ice cream layer

6 large egg yolks

75 g (2¾ oz/⅓ cup) caster (superfine) sugar

500 ml (17 fl oz/2 cups) full-cream milk

500 ml (17 fl oz/2 cups) fresh mango purée

1–1½ teaspoons fresh lime juice, or to taste

Coconut ice cream layer

400 ml (14 fl oz) tin coconut cream

125 ml (4 fl oz/½ cup) thin (pouring) cream

55 g (2 oz/¼ cup) caster (superfine) sugar

½ teaspoon pure vanilla extract

To make the mango ice cream layer, put the egg yolks and sugar in a bowl and whisk together until smooth. Heat the milk over medium–high heat until it just reaches simmering point, then cool very slightly and pour it onto the egg yolk mixture, whisking it in.

Pour the mixture into a clean saucepan and stir over medium–low heat for 10 minutes, or until the mixture thickens and coats the back of a spoon. Do not allow to boil.

Remove from the heat and stir in the mango purée and lime juice until well combined. Allow to cool, then strain through a fine sieve. Cover and refrigerate until well chilled.

To make the coconut ice cream layer, combine the coconut cream, cream, sugar and vanilla in a saucepan and stir over medium heat until the sugar has dissolved. Remove from the heat and cool. Cover and refrigerate until cold.

Set up an ice cream machine according to the manufacturer's instructions.

Add the mango mixture to the ice cream machine and churn according to the manufacturer's instructions. (Alternatively, you can pour the custard mixture into a large shallow cake tin and freeze for 2–3 hours, or until just frozen around the edges. Whisk to evenly distribute the ice crystals through the mixture. Repeat this every hour until the mixture is frozen and evenly textured.)

Line a 20 x 30 cm (8 x 12 inch) slab tin with a long piece of plastic wrap, so it hangs well over the edges of the two short ends of the tin. Spoon the mixture into the tin, then smooth the surface evenly, using a crank-handled palette knife or a spatula. Freeze for 1 hour, or until almost firm.

Clean the ice cream maker bowl and set it up again. Add the chilled coconut mixture to the ice cream machine and churn. (Alternatively, transfer to a shallow metal tray and freeze, whisking every hour or so until frozen and creamy.) Remove the tin from the freezer and spread the coconut ice cream out over the mango layer, as smoothly and evenly as possible. Evenly sprinkle the toasted coconut or macadamias over the top, if using. Return to the freezer for 2 hours, or until as firm as possible.

When ready to serve, dip the base of the tin very briefly in hot water, then place it on your bench and use the overhanging plastic to help remove the slab of ice cream from the tin, onto a cutting board.

Starting at one short end and working your way to the other, cut the slab into 2 cm (¾ inch) wide slices using a large heavy knife. Now cut in half lengthways to make 30 shorter ice cream bars, about 10 cm (4 inches) long. As each slice is removed from the slab, transfer it to a tray in the freezer. Between slices, dip your knife into boiling water, then quickly but safely dry it with a tea towel before you slice again — the hot knife will slide through more easily.

Wrap a piece of baking paper around the bottom half of each bar before serving — or serve with a plate and spoon.

To store, wrap each bar in baking paper, sealing the edges tightly, then keep in an airtight container in the fridge. The bars will keep for up to 1 week, but are best eaten within a few days of making.

Ice blocks

If there's one quick way to cool the kids down on those long hot summer days and nights, it's sucking on an ice block (or icy pop, popsicle, ice lolly, icy pole — or whatever else you call it in your neck of the woods). They are very quick, easy and reasonably cheap to make at home — and you don't need an ice cream machine! — so why not have a few ready in the freezer for the little ones and kid-ults in your life. They're also a great way to utilise an affordable glut of fresh seasonal fruit.

Makes six 90 ml (3 fl oz) ice blocks

1 quantity of your choice of the recipes on pages 102–103

Basically you'll need 540 ml (19 fl oz) of some form of liquid to fill the moulds. You can follow the ingredient quantities in the mini recipes over the page, or choose your own ingredients and experiment to your heart's delight.

Once you have made your liquid mixture (note that some will be closer to a purée than water) based on the recipes below and over the page, you need to divide the mixture among six 90 ml (3 fl oz) ice block moulds, then pop on the lids with the sticks that come with the moulds.

Some of these recipes will ask you to fill the moulds in stages for a layered look, and will freeze part of the mixture for a short time first — without the lids and sticks — but once the moulds are filled to the top, you should freeze them for 8 hours, or overnight, to ensure they are frozen solid.

To serve, you may need to dip the outside of the ice block mould very briefly in hot water, or, if serving one at a time, hold a hot clean washcloth around the outside of each ice block until it slips out of the mould. Each mould is different, so follow the manufacturer's instructions for best results.

Raspberries & cream

Put 125 g (4½ oz/1 cup) fresh or frozen raspberries in a food processor with 60 ml (2 fl oz/¼ cup) Sugar syrup (page 216) and process until smooth. Divide among six moulds and freeze for 1 hour. Combine 250 ml (9 fl oz/1 cup) thin (pouring) cream with ½ teaspoon pure vanilla extract, 1 tablespoon Sugar syrup (page 216) and 30 g (1 oz/¼ cup) very lightly crushed fresh or frozen raspberries. Divide among the moulds, over the top of the set raspberry purée. Pop the stick lids on and freeze as instructed above.

Strawberry patch

Rinse and hull 600 g (1 lb 5 oz/ 4 cups) ripe, fragrant strawberries. Cut half the strawberries into 6 mm (¼ inch) dice and place in a bowl. Purée the remaining strawberries with 125 ml (4 fl oz/½ cup) Sugar syrup (page 216). Combine the purée with the diced strawberries and add a light squeeze of lemon or lime juice to balance the flavour if needed. Fill and freeze as instructed on page 101.

Banana nut

Slice 3 small ripe bananas and place in a blender. Add 375 ml (13 fl oz/ 1½ cups) full-cream milk, ½ teaspoon pure vanilla extract and 1 tablespoon honey and process until smooth. Stir in 30 g (1 oz/¼ cup) chopped toasted macadamia nuts. Fill and freeze as instructed on page 101. After 1 hour, give each a little stir to distribute the nuts, then continue to freeze.

Choc malted

Whisk together 500 ml (17 fl oz/ 2 cups) full-cream milk, 80 ml (2½ fl oz/⅓ cup) Chocolate syrup (page 217), 30 g (1 oz/¼ cup) malted milk powder and ½ teaspoon pure vanilla extract. Fill and freeze as instructed on page 101. When you release the ice blocks from the moulds, you might like to dip the tips briefly in warm water, then into some malt powder or choc-malt powder.

flavour fancy?

Rose-melon

Combine 500 ml (17 fl oz/2 cups) fresh watermelon purée with 2 teaspoons lime juice, 1 tablespoon finely chopped fresh mint, a pinch of sea salt, ¾–1 teaspoon rosewater (or to taste), and, if needed, 1 tablespoon Sugar syrup (page 216). Fill and freeze as instructed on page 101. (For kid-ults, you could add a spash of good rum, etc…)

Guava tropicana

Mash half a ripe banana in a bowl. Add 300 ml (10½ fl oz) guava juice, 200 g (7 oz) finely diced sweet, ripe pineapple (and any juice that results from chopping), plus 90 g (3¼ oz/ ⅓ cup) passionfruit pulp (strain the pulp if you don't like seeds — but you may need to top up with a little more liquid to make the full 540 ml/ 19 fl oz). Fill the moulds and freeze as instructed on page101.

Mango cheesecake

Divide 185 ml (6 fl oz/¾ cup) fresh mango purée among six ice cream moulds. Freeze for 1 hour. To a food processor, add 150 g (5½ oz) cream cheese, 125 ml (4 fl oz/½ cup) full-cream milk, 125 ml (4 fl oz/½ cup) condensed milk, ½ teaspoon finely chopped lime zest, 1½ tablespoons lime juice, ¼ teaspoon ground cinnamon and ½ teaspoon pure vanilla extract. Process until smooth and creamy, then fill the moulds and freeze as instructed on page 101.

Chapter 3

LOLLY COUNTER

WHILE THE LOLLY counter was, for us as kids, the most important section of any milkbar, it was not uncommon to find a lolly shelf or two in a greengrocer's shop or newsagency. Lollies galore… lucky us!

In safer times, when I was around the age of six or seven, we'd walk to the shops on our own, giddy with excitement at the opportunity to select our own 'food' — how often did a kid get to do *that*? And oh what a yield we'd score with our 20 cents pocket money. The bag would be so big we could barely wrap our greedy fingers around it to stop our precious lollies falling out. If a grandparent gave us 50 cents on a special occasion, we were into serious haul quantities — that's when the stock and trade would begin.

Later, when I was walking to and from school in a group, a couple of people would distract the shop owner while someone else filled their bag, adding in a few extra cobbers, lolly teeth or milk bottles. It was an honesty system back then, you see. Clearly there was good reason why that changed. The naughtier kids would steal a whole bag of chips or a chocolate bar or a packet of bubble gum — not mentioning any names again, Vanessa…

We all had our favourites (some of us can't let go of them), and after polling many friends, family and colleagues I've included a collection of sweeties that should satisfy kids of all ages. If you're a fan of toffee-covered nuts, mint-flavoured nougat chews, twists of liquorice, crunchy honeycomb or musk sticks then we have you covered.

Musk sticks

These musk sticks taste like the ones we had as kids. A little crisp on the outside, and tender in the centre, these are the 'goldilocks' of the musk-stick world — the aroma, flavour and texture are just right. I must warn you they are rather more-ish, and all my guinea pigs agreed 'they taste like musk sticks, only better'. You can double the batch if you have a big kid's party on. Or even a big-kids' party.

Makes about 32 sticks

mild-flavoured cooking oil spray

4 small gelatine sheets (6 g/⅛ oz in total), each about 7 cm x 11.5 cm (2¾ inches x 4¼ inches)

1 tablespoon liquid glucose

½ teaspoon good-quality musk essence

a few drops of pure vanilla extract

2 drops of red food colouring (optional)

250 g (9 oz/2 cups) icing sugar mixture, sifted

Spray two baking trays with cooking oil spray. Line the trays with baking paper. (Oiling the trays first will help the baking paper sheets adhere, so they don't slip around when you're trying to pipe the musk mixture onto them.)

Soak the gelatine sheets in cold water for 5 minutes, or until soft and pliable. Drain and squeeze out the excess water.

Put the gelatine in a saucepan with the glucose and 60 ml (2 fl oz/ ¼ cup) cold water. Stir over high heat until the gelatine sheets have melted. Remove from the heat and tip into the bowl of an electric mixer fitted with a whisk attachment.

When the mixture is cool, add the musk essence, vanilla and food colouring, if using. Add 125 g (4½ oz/1 cup) of the icing sugar and beat at low speed until well combined. Increase the speed to high and whisk for 1 minute, or until smooth and evenly coloured.

Turn your machine off and add the remaining icing sugar. Mix in slowly, then increase the speed to high for about 3 minutes, to ensure it is all well incorporated, and a little like a thick, raw meringue mixture.

Put the mixture into a piping (icing) bag fitted with a 1 cm (½ inch) star-shaped nozzle and pipe 10 cm (4 inch) lengths onto the baking trays. (If your mixture is too firm to pipe, simply tip it back into the electric mixer bowl and add extra cold water, just 1 teaspoon at a time, until you have a pliable consistency. Just be careful not to add too much — a little water goes a long way in this recipe.)

Leave in a cool, dry place to set overnight. The musk sticks should be crisp and dry all the way through.

They will keep in an airtight container for several months, but will soften over time, as sugar is a fickle medium and its natural moisture content depends on the weather.

Nut brittle

I'm having a flashback to a sales assistant with a bad perm, wearing a short, patterned muumuu, her face obscured by a giant, floppy bow: from child height, this was the view at the counter of the old-school confectionery stores we used to go to.

One of my favourites from the time is this golden oldie, most commonly available in peanut form. However, you can use any nut you like the flavour of — macadamia, Brazil or cashew to name a few... and almond, pistachio, pecan, hazelnut or pine nuts, to name a few more. You may also like to lightly toast your nuts, for a deeper flavour.

If you have a nut allergy, try a mix of toasted seeds such as sunflower or sesame, or even shredded coconut.

Makes about 30 pieces

220 g (7¾ oz/1 cup) caster (superfine) sugar

2 tablespoons liquid glucose

1½ tablespoons golden syrup, light treacle or honey

1½ tablespoons butter

140 g (5 oz/1 cup) peanuts, roasted

a large pinch of fine sea salt

½ teaspoon bicarbonate of soda (baking soda)

Line a deep-sided baking tray or Swiss roll (jelly roll) tin with baking paper.

Put the sugar, glucose, golden syrup and 2 tablespoons water in a large saucepan. Stir over high heat with a metal spoon until the sugar has dissolved. Stop stirring. Bring to the boil and cook for 10 minutes, swirling the pan occasionally, until the mixture reaches an amber colour and starts to smell like toffee. Immediately stir in the butter, then mix in the peanuts and salt. Remove from the heat and stir in the bicarbonate of soda.

Pour onto the lined tray or tin and spread out a little with a spatula. Allow to cool completely, which may take a couple of hours, then break the brittle into shards.

Store in an airtight container in a cool, dark place; the brittle will keep for a month or so. Over time, the brittle may soften, or become a little sticky in humid weather — all the more reason to share it around and eat it up quickly!

The brittle is also great crushed over ice cream, or layered in a sundae, and makes a pretty golden garnish on the top of a cake.

Just add chocolate!

Dip the shards — either the edge or the whole thing — into melted chocolate of your choice, allowing any excess chocolate to drip off. Place on a tray lined with baking paper and leave until the chocolate firms up; on a hot day, you may need to set the chocolate in the fridge. If you want just a hint of chocolate, you can simply drizzle a little chocolate over the brittle pieces.

For a **sweet, salty hit**, you can sprinkle the chocolate-coated shards with a little extra sea salt.

If you're feeling nostalgic for a **scorched peanut bar**, before the brittle is fully set, cut it into even fingers about 15 cm (6 inches) long and dip the fingers into melted chocolate to coat, then leave to set.

Wonder wheels

Layer upon layer upon layer... who on earth could resist the temptation of home-made marshmallow and jam, sandwiched between two delicate buttery cookies dipped in chocolate? Seriously, snack to the max! These are adult-sized wheels, but you can make them half-size for kids, as they're quite rich. Roll on over the page to check out all the different variations.

Makes 6 large wheels

½ quantity of Marshmallow (page 117); see Note

6 teaspoons good-quality raspberry, strawberry or cherry jam

150 g (5½ oz) 70% dark chocolate

150 g (5½ oz) good-quality milk chocolate

30 g (1 oz) Copha (white vegetable shortening) or solid coconut oil

Biscuit dough

200 g (7 oz) unsalted butter

125 g (4½ oz/1 cup) icing (confectioners') sugar

300 g (10½ oz/2 cups) plain (all-purpose) flour

pinch of sea salt

1 egg yolk

½ teaspoon pure vanilla extract

Start by making the biscuit dough. Cut the butter into 2 cm (¾ inch) dice and chill. Put the icing sugar, flour and salt in a food processor and process quickly to combine. Put the egg yolk, vanilla and 1 teaspoon water in a small jug and mix with a fork to combine. Add the chilled butter to the processor and pulse until the mixture becomes crumb-like. With the motor running, gradually add the egg mixture until the dough just comes together.

Remove the dough from the processor, gather into a ball, then flatten to a thick disc. Wrap in plastic wrap and refrigerate for 1 hour.

Line two baking trays with baking paper. Roll the dough out on a lightly floured surface to a thickness of about 4 mm (³⁄₁₆ inch). Use a 9 cm (3½ inch) cookie cutter to cut 12 rounds from the dough, transferring them to the baking trays. Place the trays in the fridge and chill the dough again for 30 minutes.

Preheat the oven to 180°C (350°F). Bake the biscuit rounds for about 10 minutes, or until evenly golden, then transfer to wire racks to cool.

Now use an 8 cm (3¼ inch) cookie cutter, dipped in hot water if needed, to cut out marshmallow rounds, then transfer to the top of half the biscuits. Spread a thin layer of jam over the remaining biscuits, not quite taking it to the edges. Place these on top of the marshmallow rounds, jam side down, and press gently until the marshmallow ends up even with the

biscuit edges. It may shrink back a little, but that's okay!

Melt all the chocolate and the Copha in a heatproof bowl set over a saucepan of simmering water, ensuring the base of the bowl doesn't touch the water. Stir occasionally until almost completely melted, then remove from the heat and continue to stir until very smooth and liquid. The mixture should be no warmer than body temperature when you dip the biscuit sandwiches in.

Using a fork or a crank-handled palette knife, carefully lower the biscuit sandwiches into the chocolate mixture, ensuring they are completely covered. Remove, allowing any excess chocolate to drip back into the bowl, and transfer to trays lined with baking paper. Chill for several hours, or until the coating is well set.

Your wheels are best eaten within a few days, but will last up to 1 week in a sealed container in the fridge.

NOTE *If taking the marshmallow from a whole quantity of the recipe, use a hot, wet knife to cut the marshmallow sheet horizontally in half, to give two thinner sheets; just use one of these sheets in this recipe. If you make just half the quantity fresh in the same sized tin as the full recipe, you'll have one marshmallow sheet of the right thickness.*

PAINT YOUR WAGON!

Put your own stamp on your Wonder wheels (see previous page) by changing the biscuit, jam, marshmallow flavour and chocolate type. Here are a few ideas to get you started.

Peachy keen

Use Raspberry marshmallow (see Strawberry marshmallow, page 118) + peach jam + white chocolate.

Minted wagon

Use Peppermint marshmallow (see Essence and liqueur-flavoured marshmallow, page 118) + blackberry jam + dark chocolate.

Couldn't give a fig

Replace some of the flour in the biscuits with almond or hazelnut meal. Use Coffee marshmallow (page 118) + fig jam + caramelised white chocolate (from the Caramel buds recipe on page 127).

Lemon & spice

Add ground cinnamon and ginger to the basic biscuit mix. Use Lemon marshmallow (see Strawberry marshmallow, page 118) + white chocolate.

Strawberry fields

Use Strawberry marshmallow (page 118) + strawberry jam + white chocolate. Sprinkle the tops with toasted coconut + crumbled freeze-dried strawberries.

Gone troppo

Add a little finely chopped glacé ginger in the biscuit mix. Use pineapple jam + Passionfruit marshmallow (see Strawberry marshmallow, page 118) + half dark/half milk chocolate.

Gingernutmegs

Add a little ground ginger and freshly grated nutmeg to the biscuit mix. Use Lemon marshmallow (see Strawberry marshmallow, page 118) + apricot jam + dark chocolate.

Fizzy sherbet powder

A purely nostalgic addition. If you are a child of the 1970s, you may remember those little opaque paper bags of sherbet, sold with a teensy spoon? First you licked your spoon, then dipped it into the bag so the powder would cling to it, then put it in your mouth, and repeated until all the sweet, fizzy, powdered sugar had gone and you were in a bit of a daze. An inexpensive but thrilling high. It was the same kind of fizzy stuff that filled sherbet cones, which were like a mini ice cream cone, but topped with marshmallow coated in hundreds and thousands. There were also sherbet fountains, with a liquorice straw for sucking up the fizz, small chewy lollies with fizzy centres, sherbet-filled straws and sherbet flying saucers! (In Australia there was also another popular Sherbet, with a filling of Daryl Braithwaite, cloaked in snug satin suits. Good times. Howzat!) A nice way to give the kids just a taste of this fun treat — and I stress the words *fun* and *treat* — is to sprinkle a little over cut fruit.

Makes 10 (1 tablespoon) packets, or 20 (2 teaspoon) serves

2½ teaspoons citric acid

2¼ teaspoons bicarbonate of soda (baking soda)

120 g (4¼ oz/1 cup) icing sugar mixture

Mix all the ingredients in a bowl until well combined. If not using straight away, store in a small airtight container; the mixture is best used within a week.

For serving, divide among small paper bags or mini cups. Kids can dip into the sherbet with a finger, spoon, lollipop, liquorice strap or a piece of fruit.

CHANGE THE FLAVOUR *by adding some dehydrated fruit powder or jelly crystals.*

Marshmallow

The word 'marshmallow' conjures whimsical imagery of sweet youth, does it not? Airy pillows of fanciful delight. This recipe and the flavour variations on the next page are guaranteed to turn you away from supermarket versions for life.

I suggest making marshmallows on cooler, less humid days — when working with sugar, the weather can play a big part in the final outcome. Sugar can be a sticky trickster like that.

Makes about 50 pieces

mild-flavoured cooking oil spray

20 g (¾ oz) gelatine sheets (12 sheets, each 7 x 11.5 cm/2¾ x 4¼ inches)

1 tablespoon pure vanilla extract

375 ml (13 fl oz/1½ cups) cold water

250 ml (9 fl oz/1 cup) liquid glucose

1½ tablespoons honey

275 g (9¾ oz/1¼ cups) caster (superfine) sugar

For coating

125 g (4½ oz/1 cup) icing sugar mixture, sifted

125 g (4½ oz/1 cup) cornflour (cornstarch), sifted

Spray a 20 x 30 cm (8 x 12 inch) baking tin evenly with cooking oil spray.

Soak the gelatine sheets in cold water for 5 minutes, or until softened. Squeeze out any excess liquid, then place in the bowl of an electric mixer. Add the vanilla and 125 ml (4 fl oz/½ cup) of the water. Attach the whisk attachment to the mixer and gently mix the gelatine and liquids together.

Pour the remaining water into a saucepan with a pouring lip. Add the glucose, honey and caster sugar and stir over medium heat until the sugar has just dissolved. After this point, do not stir at all. Use a pastry brush dipped in water to run around the inside rim of the pan to ensure there are no sugar crystals lurking. Increase the heat to high and boil until the syrup reaches 120°C (248°F) on a sugar thermometer. Immediately remove from the heat.

Turn the electric mixer onto medium–low speed. Pouring carefully, gradually add the hot sugar syrup to the gelatine mixture in a stream. Once the gelatine mixture has melted, you can add the rest of the syrup more quickly. Cover the top of the bowl with a tea towel to collect any splatters if you like and increase the speed to high. Whisk continuously on high for 20–25 minutes — make sure you go the whole distance, as the time is needed to cool and stabilise the marshmallow. You will end up with a thick, glossy, fluffy mass, like soft-peak meringue.

Use a spatula to scrape the marshmallow into your baking tin and very gently smooth over. Leave to set at room temperature for at least 6 hours, but ideally overnight if you can, to let the texture and flavour settle. If it is a really hot, humid day, set the marshmallow in the fridge.

When ready to coat the marshmallow, combine the icing sugar mixture and cornflour and sprinkle a little on a clean work surface. To release the marshmallow from the tin, you may need to run a hot, wet knife around the inside edge of the tin. Sprinkle some icing sugar mixture over the top of the marshmallow and smooth over with your hands. Turn the marshmallow out onto your work surface, sprinkle more of the mixture over the top and smooth over.

Using a sharp knife, cut the marshmallow into 3 cm x 4 cm (1¼ inch x 1½ inch) rectangles. Dip any exposed marshmallow edges in the remaining icing sugar mixture.

Store your marshmallows in an airtight container to keep the moisture out. To stop them sticking together, stack them in single layers, sprinkling each layer with any leftover icing sugar mixture, and placing a sheet of baking paper between each layer.

They will keep in a cool dark place (or in the fridge in warm weather) for up to 1 week. They will start to break down a little after this time, and not look so pretty, but will still taste good.

NOTE *Try flavouring the marshmallow with essences or fruit juice of your choice (see next page for examples); omit or reduce the vanilla. Note that the acid and enzymes in some fruits, particularly tropical varieties, can 'eat' into the gelatine and stop it setting quite as well, so in these cases try using heat-treated bottled juice, or briefly boil fresh fruit juice. If in doubt, you can add a little more gelatine — just be aware the consistency may differ from fruit to fruit.*

MARSH MADNESS

Toasted coconut-coated marshmallow

Before the marshmallow goes into the baking tin, scatter about 90 g (3¼ oz/ 1 cup) toasted desiccated or shredded coconut evenly across the tin. Carefully pour in the marshmallow mixture, then sprinkle another 65 g (2½ oz/1 cup) toasted coconut evenly over the top. After the marshmallow has set, cut into pieces and dip the exposed cut edges into another 65 g (2½ oz/1 cup) toasted coconut. There is no need to coat it in the icing sugar and cornflour mix.

Coffee marshmallow

When adding the vanilla to the pre-soaked gelatine in the mixer bowl, instead of adding 125 ml (4 fl oz/½ cup) water, add 125 ml (4 fl oz/½ cup) strong espresso coffee, then follow the rest of the recipe.

Essence and liqueur-flavoured marshmallow

You can drop back the vanilla if you are adding other flavours. Once the marshmallow mixture has been beaten for the full 20–25 minutes, beat in a little of your favourite essence or liqueur. Start with the 'less is more approach' and build up to the flavour you desire, as different ingredients vary in strength — for example, I use 1–1½ tablespoons **rosewater** per batch, but only 1–2 teaspoons **peppermint extract**. You may need to add 2 tablespoons of your favourite liqueur to get the flavour through.

Mocha marshmallow

When adding the vanilla to the pre-soaked gelatine in the mixer bowl, instead of adding 125 ml (4 fl oz/½ cup) water, add 125 ml (4 fl oz/½ cup) strong espresso coffee, and 1½ tablespoons good-quality unsweetened cocoa powder. Follow the rest of the recipe as instructed.

Strawberry marshmallow

Replace 250 ml (9 fl oz/1 cup) of the total amount of water with 250 ml (9 fl oz/1 cup) fresh strawberry juice. (You can use a juice extractor to make the juice, or you can purée the strawberries, then sieve to remove any pulp — you just want pure juice.) Add 125 ml (4 fl oz/½ cup) of the strawberry juice to the pre-soaked gelatine in the mixer bowl; cut back on the vanilla a little, to allow the fruit flavour to shine. When making the hot sugar syrup, reduce the water to 125 ml (4 fl oz/½ cup) and add the remaining 125 ml (4 fl oz/½ cup) strawberry juice. Follow the rest of the recipe as instructed. Experiment with other juices too, such as **raspberry**, **passionfruit**, **orange** and **lemon**; see the note on page 117.

Coconut ice

If you find coconut ice overly sweet, try this version — it's a little more creamy and less sugary than most. Instead of vanilla extract, you can also use rosewater, orange blossom water, peppermint extract or musk essence, and adjust the colour accordingly — for example by using green food colouring instead of red for a peppermint coconut ice. Or simply leave it *au naturel*.

Makes 64 pieces

mild-flavoured cooking oil spray

300 g (10½ oz) icing (confectioners') sugar

¼ teaspoon cream of tartar

270 g (9½ oz/3 cups) desiccated coconut

315 g (11¼ oz/1 cup) condensed milk

50 g (1¾ oz) Copha (white vegetable shortening) or solid coconut oil, melted and cooled slightly

1 teaspoon pure vanilla extract

3–4 drops of red or pink food colouring (optional)

Lightly spray a 20 cm (8 inch) square cake tin with cooking oil spray. Line the base and two sides with baking paper, so that it overhangs on two sides — this will help to lift the confectionery out of the tin once it has set.

Sift the icing sugar and cream of tartar into a bowl and combine. Stir in the coconut until well combined, then make a well in the centre. Pour in the condensed milk, Copha and vanilla and stir until thoroughly combined.

If you would rather avoid using food colouring, simply spoon the mixture into the cake tin, smoothing it over. Cover with plastic wrap and chill for 4 hours, or until set.

If you would like a traditional two-toned effect, divide the mixture between two bowls. Add a couple of drops of food colouring to one bowl and mix until the colour is even. Spoon the plain mixture into the cake tin and smooth over, then top with the pink mixture and smooth over. Cover and chill until set.

To serve, use the overhanging baking paper to help you lift the coconut ice from the tin. Use a sharp knife to cut into 2.5 cm (1 inch) squares.

Store in an airtight container in the fridge; the coconut ice will keep for up to 1 month.

Twice as nice!

Choc cherry coconut ice

Drop the desiccated coconut back to 210 g (7½ oz/2⅓ cups), and add 160 g (5¾ oz/⅔ cup) finely chopped glacé cherries. Omit the food colouring, if you like. When set, drizzle the top with melted chocolate and allow it to set again, before cutting into squares.

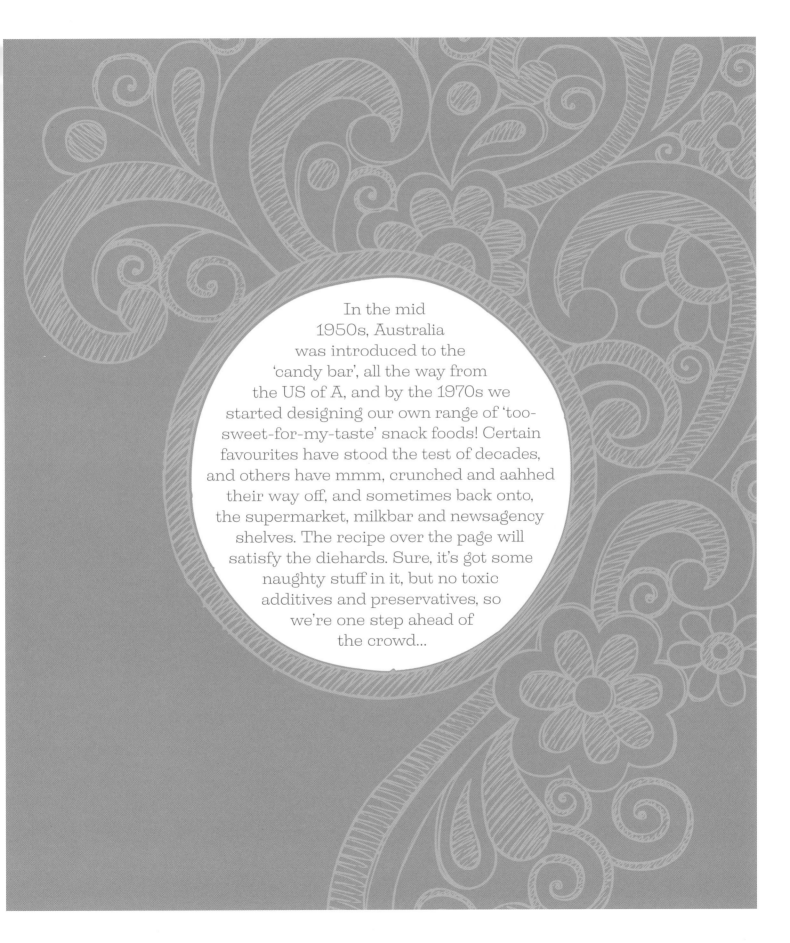

In the mid 1950s, Australia was introduced to the 'candy bar', all the way from the US of A, and by the 1970s we started designing our own range of 'too-sweet-for-my-taste' snack foods! Certain favourites have stood the test of decades, and others have mmm, crunched and aahhed their way off, and sometimes back onto, the supermarket, milkbar and newsagency shelves. The recipe over the page will satisfy the diehards. Sure, it's got some naughty stuff in it, but no toxic additives and preservatives, so we're one step ahead of the crowd...

Nougat caramel candy bars

I'm quietly confident that these home-made bars will never fade into oblivion. By cutting them into bite-sized bars before dipping in chocolate, you can control the kids' consumption. Adults, on the other hand... well you're on your own there.

Makes 20 bars about 10 cm (4 inches) long, or 40 mini bars

mild-flavoured cooking
  oil spray

Nutty nougat layer

175 g (6 oz/½ cup) honey

440 g (15½ oz/2 cups) caster
  (superfine) sugar

435 ml (15¼ fl oz/1¾ cups)
  liquid glucose

2 egg whites

a pinch of sea salt

50 g (1¾ oz) unsalted butter,
  melted

1 teaspoon pure vanilla
  extract

2 tablespoons malted milk
  powder

70 g (2½ oz/½ cup) nuts of your
  choice, toasted and roughly
  chopped (optional)

Chewy caramel layer

330 g (11¾ oz/1½ cups)
  caster (superfine) or
  golden caster sugar

3 tablespoons golden syrup
  or light treacle

125 ml (4 fl oz/½ cup) thin
  (pouring) cream

60 g (2¼ oz) unsalted butter

a good pinch of sea salt

Chocolate coating

250 g (9 oz) 70% dark
  chocolate, chopped

250 g (9 oz) good-quality milk
  chocolate, chopped

Lightly spray a 20 x 30 cm (8 x 12 inch) slab tin with cooking oil spray. Line with a long strip of baking paper, letting it overhang two sides, to make it easier to remove the confectionery once it has set. Lightly spray the baking paper too.

To make the nougat layer

Put the honey and 2½ tablespoons water in a saucepan. Add 110 g (3¾ oz/½ cup) of the sugar, and 60 ml (2 fl oz/¼ cup) of the liquid glucose. Stir over high heat until the sugar has dissolved. Run a wet pastry brush around the inside edge of the pan to dissolve any sugar crystals that may be stuck to the side.

Bring to the boil, without stirring, until the mixture reaches 120°C (248°F) on your sugar thermometer.

Meanwhile, place the egg whites and salt in the bowl of a heavy-duty standing mixer and beat at high speed until stiff peaks form.

When the sugar syrup reaches 120°C (248°F), remove from the heat. With the mixer motor running at full speed, carefully run a thin stream of the hot sugar syrup down the side of the bowl; as it starts to thicken up you can add it in a more steady stream. When all the sugar syrup has been added, keep beating for a further 5 minutes, or until the mixture is very thick.

While the mixture is beating, put the remaining 375 ml (13 fl oz/1½ cups) liquid glucose and remaining 330 g (11¾ oz/1½ cups) caster sugar in a saucepan with 60 ml (2 fl oz/¼ cup) water. Stir with a metal spoon over high heat until the sugar has dissolved, then do not stir again. Run a wet pastry brush around the inside edge of the pan to dissolve any sugar crystals that may have formed. Bring to 138°C (280°F) and immediately remove from the heat.

With the motor on your standing mixer running at full speed, carefully run a thin stream of the hot liquid down the side of the bowl; as the mixture starts to fluff up you can add it in a more steady stream. Once all the sugar has been combined, add the warm melted butter, vanilla and malt powder and mix on medium speed for 5 minutes. The mixture will lose a fair amount of air and become more liquid — this is meant to happen, so don't worry. Remove the bowl from the mixer. Using a wooden spoon or stiff spatula, stir in the nuts, if using.

Pour into the slab tin. Smooth over with a crank-handled palette knife that has been dipped in hot water. Refrigerate for 1 hour, or until cold and firm to the touch.

To make the caramel layer

Put the sugar and golden syrup in a saucepan with 125 ml (4 fl oz/½ cup) water. Stir over medium–high heat with a metal spoon until the sugar has dissolved. Bring to the boil and cook, without stirring, until the mixture reaches 140–145°C (284–293°F) on a sugar thermometer, swirling the pan occasionally to promote even, dark-golden caramelisation; it will smell like toffee. Remove from the heat and use a long-handled metal spoon to stir in the cream, butter and salt until smooth. Cool slightly, then pour over the top of the nougat layer in the tin, tilting the tin to ensure the caramel reaches the very edges. Cover the top of the tin with plastic wrap, ensuring it doesn't touch the caramel, and refrigerate overnight.

The next day, use the overhanging strips of paper to lift the mixture from the tin, onto a cutting board. Place the short ends of the slab left and right. Using a sharp, heavy knife dipped in hot water, cut into 3 cm (1¼ inch) wide vertical strips, then cut lengthways through them all, to form 20 bars, each about 10 cm (4 inches) long. If you like, you can cut the bars in half again, into 5 cm (2 inch) mini bars, as they are quite rich. Place on a tray and freeze for 3 hours.

For the chocolate coating

Melt two-thirds of all the chocolate in a heatproof bowl set over a saucepan of simmering water, ensuring the base of the bowl doesn't touch the water. Stir occasionally with a metal spoon until almost completely melted, then remove from the heat and continue to stir until very smooth and liquid. Add the remaining chocolate and stir until melted. Keep the saucepan of water simmering gently in case you need to warm the chocolate again during dipping.

Remove the bars from the freezer, just a few at a time, and use a fork to help you dip each bar into the melted chocolate, allowing any excess to drip off. Place on a tray lined with baking paper. Repeat until all the bars are covered. If the chocolate becomes too firm, briefly place it back over the simmering pan, just until liquid again. Place the tray of bars in the fridge and leave to set for about 1 hour, or until dry to the touch.

Before serving, allow the bars to sit out of the fridge for 5–10 minutes, to soften the caramel and nougat slightly.

Store in an airtight container, layered between sheets of baking paper. The bars will keep in the fridge for 2–3 weeks; they also freeze well for up to 1 month, before the sugar starts to break down; the frozen bars are easier to bite into than the refrigerated ones, which are sticky and chewy.

Rocky road

A cheap rocky road makes me want to cry, but give me a home-made slab created with quality ingredients and I'm your friend for life. Some great boutique rocky roads are available these days, but given it is so easy (and often cheaper) to make your own, why wouldn't you just whip up a batch? Plus you can design it to include all the goodies you love! Rocky road traditionally contains peanuts, glacé cherries, marshmallow and coconut in milk chocolate, but I like to come up with different combinations depending on my mood, or whoever I'm making it for (see next page for ideas). Rocky road also keeps well (if not in my possession) and makes a great gift, especially when times are rocky... What's a little comfort eating between friends?

Makes four 20 cm (8 inch) logs, or 32 pieces

mild-flavoured cooking oil spray

200 g (7 oz) Marshmallow (about a ⅓ quantity of the recipe on page 117), in any flavour of your choice, cut into 3 cm x 4 cm (1¼ inch x 1½ inch) pieces

100 g (3½ oz/½ cup) glacé fruit, such as cherries, apricots, figs or ginger, chopped into 1.5 cm (⅝ inch) squares

140 g (5 oz/1 cup) nuts of your choice, lightly toasted, then roughly chopped

50 g (1¾ oz/⅔ cup) shredded coconut, toasted

400 g (14 oz) good-quality dark, milk or white chocolate, chopped

Spray a 20 cm (8 inch) square cake tin with cooking oil spray. Line the tin with a long strip of baking paper, letting it overhang two sides, to make it easier to lift out the rocky road once it has set.

Put the marshmallow, glacé fruit, nuts and coconut in a bowl and gently combine using your hands.

Place the chocolate in a heatproof bowl set over a saucepan of simmering water, ensuring the base of the bowl doesn't touch the water. Stir the chocolate regularly until just melted and smooth. Remove from the heat. The melted chocolate should be barely warm at all — if it is, simply leave for a minute.

Pour the melted chocolate over the marshmallow mixture. Use a large spoon or spatula to gently combine all the ingredients, ensuring they are evenly coated in the chocolate.

Tip the mixture into your cake tin, then gently and evenly distribute the mixture with a spatula. Refrigerate for 4 hours, or until completely set.

Remove the rocky road from the tin, using your baking paper handles. Cut into four logs, about 5 cm (2 inch) wide and 20 cm (8 inch) long. You can wrap these to give as gifts, or you can slice each log into eight pieces and enjoy with a cuppa!

To store, wrap the whole rocky road, or pieces of it, in plastic wrap or baking paper and keep in an airtight container. It will last in the fridge for up to 1 month.

ALONG THE ROCKY PATH...

Road to Istanbul

Dark chocolate + Rosewater marshmallow (see Essence and liqueur-flavoured marshmallow, page 118) + Turkish delight (page 142) + pistachio nuts + toasted sesame seeds.

Spice road

White chocolate + Marshmallow (page 117) + Crystallised ginger (page 141) + slivered almonds + ground cardamom + ground cinnamon + ground allspice.

Yuletide road

Milk chocolate + Marshmallow (page 117) + glacé figs and currants mixed with a tiny splash of rum + Crystallised ginger (page 141) + glacé cherries + mixed spice + walnuts + pecans.

Road to paradise

White chocolate + Passionfruit marshmallow (see Strawberry marshmallow, page 118) + macadamia nuts + glacé pineapple + toasted coconut.

Dark & mysterious road

Dark chocolate + Coffee marshmallow (page 118) + hazelnuts + glacé mixed peel.

A bump in the road

Milk chocolate + popping candy + Strawberry marshmallow (page 118) + jelly beans + broken-up biscuits from the Wonder wheels recipe on page 113.

Fast road to Roma

Dark and milk chocolate + broken amaretti biscuits + Orange marshmallow (see Strawberry marshmallow, page 118) + toasted almonds + candied chestnuts.

Fragrant grove road

White chocolate + Lemon marshmallow (see Strawberry marshmallow, page 118) + glacé apricot + toasted macadamia nuts.

Caramel buds

These caramel-flavoured chocolate drops were one of my favourite childhood sweets, and I'd always wondered how they were made. After a little experimenting I discovered I could make them by caramelising white chocolate (an idea I stole from my friends at Burch & Purchese Sweet Studio in Melbourne), adjusting the intensity of the caramel simply by cooking it longer. So simple and so very satisfying — trust me, your friends will be begging you for the recipe.

This recipe makes a decent batch — firstly because it is easier to work with that way, and secondly because... well I think you know why.

Makes about 64 buds

300 g (10½ oz) white chocolate (the higher cocoa butter, the better — look for 30% or more)

35 g (1¼ oz) Copha (white vegetable shortening) or solid coconut oil

a few drops of pure vanilla extract (optional)

Preheat the oven to 110°C (225°F). Line a deep-sided baking tray or Swiss roll (jelly roll) tin with baking paper.

Chop the chocolate and Copha and place on the baking tray. Transfer to the oven and cook for 10 minutes, or until the chocolate has started to melt. Give it a good stir with a silicone spatula and smooth over. Return to the oven for a further 10 minutes and repeat the stirring.

Repeat this process another five or six times, until the mixture becomes a light caramel colour and has a good toasty flavour. Quickly stir in the vanilla, if using.

Line another tray with baking paper. Holding a teaspoon vertically straight, and close to the baking tray, drop teaspoons of the melted chocolate onto the tray, to form neat button shapes, making sure there is a small gap between each button. Allow to cool slightly, then refrigerate for a few hours until completely cold.

Store in an airtight container in the fridge. The caramel buds will keep for several months (yeah, right)…

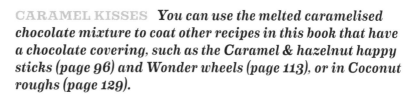

CARAMEL KISSES *You can use the melted caramelised chocolate mixture to coat other recipes in this book that have a chocolate covering, such as the Caramel & hazelnut happy sticks (page 96) and Wonder wheels (page 113), or in Coconut roughs (page 129).*

Speckles

These eye-catching sweets, covered with tiny, brightly coloured baubles of sugar, have been delighting children for several decades. You can make them in the more usual bite-sized rounds, as in the recipe below, or as fun giant-sized speckles, great for gifting.

Makes about 24 bite-sized rounds

300 g (10½ oz) milk, dark or white chocolate; the better the quality, the better your speckles will taste (and the better they'll be for you, too!)

150 g (5½ oz/½ cup) hundreds and thousands, sprinkles or cachous

Line two baking trays with baking paper and set aside.

Melt the chocolate in a heatproof bowl set over a saucepan of simmering water, ensuring the base of the bowl doesn't touch the water. Stir occasionally until the chocolate has almost completely melted, then remove from the heat and continue to stir until very smooth and liquid.

Holding a teaspoon vertically straight, and close to the baking trays, drop teaspoons of the melted chocolate onto the trays, to form neat button shapes, making sure there is a small gap between each button. While still wet, sprinkle the hundreds and thousands over the top of each button to evenly cover them.

Allow to cool slightly, then refrigerate for about 2 hours, or until cold.

Store in an airtight container in the fridge or a cool, dark place. They will keep for up to 2 months.

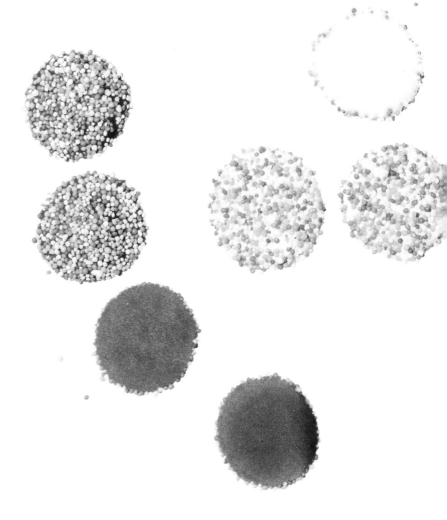

Coconut roughs

Coconut and chocolate is an eternally popular duo — just ask any lamington fan! As a child, I was curiously drawn to milkbar coconut roughs, especially when they came wrapped in shiny gold paper — call me gullible and shallow if you will. This recipe is an absolute doddle and just as perfect with an after-school glass of milk as a post-dinner coffee. And if coconut doesn't float your boat, try out the other options below.

Makes about 16

300 g (10½ oz) good-quality milk, dark or white chocolate

150 g (5½ oz) lightly toasted desiccated or shredded coconut

Melt the chocolate in a heatproof bowl set over a saucepan of simmering water, ensuring the base of the bowl doesn't touch the water. Stir occasionally with a metal spoon until almost completely melted, then remove from the heat and continue to stir until evenly smooth and liquid. Stir in the coconut.

Drop about 1 tablespoon of the mixture onto a tray lined with baking paper. Flatten to a disc about 7 cm (2¾ inches) in diameter, and about 3 mm (⅛ inch) thick. If you are a neat freak, you can use a 7 cm (2¾ inch) cookie cutter to help trim off any misshapen bits.

Refrigerate until set, then store in an airtight container in the fridge or a cool, dark place. The coconut roughs will keep for up to 2 months.

Rough diamonds

Cherry roughs

Reduce the coconut to 75 g (2¾ oz), and add 90 g (3¼ oz) finely chopped glacé cherries to the chocolate.

Ginger roughs

Reduce the coconut to 75 g (2¾ oz), and add 90 g (3¼ oz) finely chopped glacé ginger or Crystallised ginger (page 141) to the chocolate.

Sesame roughs

Instead of the coconut, use 100 g (3½ oz/⅔ cup) lightly toasted sesame seeds.

Rough nuts

Instead of the coconut, use 150 g (5½ oz) finely chopped, lightly toasted nuts of your choice, such as macadamias, almonds or Brazil nuts.

Chewy mints

Nana Doris always carried a packet of peppermints in her handbag. Mint became a flavour of comfort, as we'd be offered one whenever we felt carsick, tired or sad and it always perked us up. These ones are super minty, and super chewy.

Makes about 100

mild-flavoured cooking oil spray

295 g (10½ oz/1⅓ cups) caster (superfine) sugar

375 ml (13 fl oz/1½ cups) liquid glucose

1 extra-large egg white; you'll need 53 g (1¾ oz) egg white (see Note)

a pinch of sea salt

35 g (1¼ oz) unsalted butter, melted

1–1¼ teaspoons peppermint extract

Lightly spray a 20 cm (8 inch) square cake tin with cooking oil spray. Line with a long strip of baking paper, letting it overhang two sides, to make it easier to remove the candy once it has set. Smooth the paper into the tin. Lightly spray the baking paper.

Put the sugar, liquid glucose and 2 tablespoons water in a saucepan and stir over high heat until the sugar has dissolved. Run a wet pastry brush around the inside edge of the pan to dissolve any sugar crystals stuck to the side. Bring to the boil, without stirring, until the mixture reaches 115°C (239°F) on a sugar thermometer.

Meanwhile, place the egg white and salt in the bowl of a heavy-duty electric standing mixer and beat at high speed until stiff peaks form.

You now need to add the sugar syrup to the egg white in two stages. When the sugar mixture reaches 115°C (239°F), remove from the heat. With the motor running at full speed on your standing mixer, carefully run a thin stream of the hot sugar syrup down the side of the bowl. As it starts to thicken up, you can add it in a steady stream — but you should only use half the sugar syrup at this time. Set the rest aside, you will need it soon. Keep beating for a further 15 minutes, or until very thick.

Place the reserved sugar syrup on the heat and bring to 145°C (293°F). With the motor running on your electric mixer, use the same method as before to whisk in all the remaining sugar syrup. Keep beating

for another 10 minutes or so, until you have a thick, stiff meringue. It should have cooled down a fair bit, but will still be quite warm.

Beat in the melted butter and peppermint extract until well combined; the mixture will deflate a little, but that's okay. Pour into the cake tin, then smooth over with a wet crank-handled palette knife. Chill for a short time — until just firm, but not so hard you can't cut through it.

Cut into 1.5 x 2.5 cm (⅝ x 1 inch) rectangles. Place on a tray lined with baking paper, spaced slightly apart, and chill for about 1 hour, until completely hard.

Wrap in small squares of baking paper (don't use cellophane or they may stick), twisting each end so they look like bonbons.

Store in an airtight container in the fridge in warm weather, or a cool, dark place in cooler weather. They will keep for several months, but in humid weather they will soften as the sugar starts to break down. If stored in the freezer they shatter nicely on biting into them, then melt into a luscious chew.

NOTE *This recipe needs the correct amount of egg white. If you don't have an extra-large egg, you can use two 60 g (2¼ oz eggs), separate the whites and combine them, then weigh out 53 g (1¾ oz) of the egg white and discard the rest.*

Liquorice twists

There was always liquorice in our house, but I never liked it until deep into my adult years.

This liquorice is naturally dark brown, not black like the shop-bought variety; you can add a few drops of black food colouring if you really must.

Makes 30 long twists

mild-flavoured cooking oil spray

2 tablespoons mild-flavoured oil

185 g (6½ oz/1 cup) brown sugar

90 g (3¼ oz/¼ cup) golden syrup or light treacle

175 g (6 oz/½ cup) blackstrap molasses (from health food stores)

3½ teaspoons ground liquorice root

3½ teaspoons ground aniseed

½ teaspoon fine sea salt

225 g (8 oz/1½ cups) plain (all-purpose) flour

Line a 20 x 30 cm (8 x 12 inch) slab tin with baking paper. Lightly spray the paper with cooking oil spray to prevent sticking. Set aside.

In a large saucepan, combine the oil, sugar, golden syrup, molasses, liquorice root, aniseed and salt and stir over high heat until the sugar has dissolved.

Bring to the boil without stirring, then insert a sugar thermometer and leave to boil until the temperature reaches 110–115°C (230–239°F).

Remove the pan from the heat and gradually stir in the flour, mixing with a whisk until very well combined — check for lumps! You should end up with a thick, but still pourable, paste.

Pour the mixture into the slab tin. Smooth over with a wet palette knife and refrigerate for 30 minutes. The liquorice mixture will be firm, but not too hard to cut through at this stage.

For this next step, you'll need to work quite quickly; the warmer your kitchen, the more quickly the liquorice will become trickier to work with. So, remove the liquorice from the fridge. Using a sharp knife, and starting at a short end, cut the liquorice into thin straps, about 1 cm (½ inch) wide. Separate the straps and, working quickly from one end to another, twist them into a rope; you can then cut into smaller pieces if you like.

The straps still need to be fairly cold when you twist them — when they start to warm up, they stretch too much, and don't hold their shape. If you need to, you can put them back in the fridge for a short time to firm up again — but if they get too cold they will be too difficult to work with, so you might have to play it by ear a little, depending on the weather and the temperature of your fridge.

Place the finished twists back on a tray lined with baking paper, spaced apart so they don't stick together. Place back in the fridge to firm up.

Store in a sealed container in the fridge, stacked in layers separated by baking paper. The liquorice will keep for a couple of months.

If you don't like them too chewy, take them out of the fridge shortly before you serve them so they soften up a little.

Honeycomb

A good honeycomb should shatter easily, and not be too sticky or cloying. Humidity can play havoc with honeycomb, so don't be surprised if the end result varies depending on when and where you make it. Sticking to cooler days with less moisture in the air will yield a better result. But who am I kidding – honeycomb is pretty damn good at any time. Especially when covered in chocolate.

Makes about 40 pieces

300 g (10½ oz/1⅓ cups) caster (superfine) sugar

3 tablespoons honey, or use half honey and half golden syrup or maple syrup

125 ml (4 fl oz/½ cup) liquid glucose

a pinch of sea salt

3 teaspoons bicarbonate of soda (baking soda)

Grease a 20 x 30 cm (8 x 12 inch) slab tin and line it with a long strip of baking paper, letting it overhang two sides, to make it easier to lift the honeycomb out of the tin once it has set.

Dig out a large deep saucepan; when making honeycomb, a pan with deep sides is safer than using a wide, shallow one. Add the sugar, honey, glucose, salt and 2½ tablespoons water. Stir over medium–high heat until the sugar has completely dissolved. If there are any sugar crystals on the side of your pan, just run a wet pastry brush around the pan to dissolve them.

Now bring to the boil over high heat and cook, without stirring, until the mixture reaches about 150°C (302°F) on a sugar thermometer, swirling the pan occasionally to ensure even caramelisation. The mixture should be an even amber colour. Be careful not to take it too far at this point, or your honeycomb will taste burnt — although a little hint of 'burnt toffee' flavour is okay, as you also don't want it to taste too sweet.

Immediately remove from the heat. Using a long-handled whisk — and taking care as the mixture will rapidly expand and foam — add the bicarbonate of soda, whisking well.

Pour into the slab tin and tilt the tin around so the honeycomb covers the base as evenly as possible — don't try to smooth it over with a spoon, or you'll flatten the honeycomb; it will naturally flatten a little anyway. Allow to cool completely at room temperature.

Remove from the tin, using the baking paper handles to help you, then cut or break into pieces.

Store in an airtight container in a cool dark place or in the fridge; the honeycomb will keep for several weeks.

TOP OF THE POPS *Cover the honeycomb with 350 g (12 oz) melted chocolate of your choice; once the chocolate has set, store the honeycomb in the fridge. While the chocolate is still wet, you could even sprinkle some garnishes over, such as edible lavender, finely ground coffee, chopped toasted nuts, dried citrus peel or chopped Crystallised ginger (page 141).*

Salted caramel cobbers

'Cobber' is an archaic Aussie term for a mate, or friend. It's also the name of an old-fashioned chocolate-coated sweet, often with a firm, chewy, caramel core. True to its namesake, a cobber will never let you down.

Makes about 100 cobbers, 2 cm (¾ inch) in size

mild-flavoured cooking
  oil spray

440 g (15½ oz/2 cups) caster
  (superfine) sugar

170 ml (5½ fl oz/⅔ cup) liquid
  glucose

1½ tablespoons golden syrup
  or light treacle

250 ml (9 fl oz/1 cup) thin
  (pouring) cream

½ teaspoon pure vanilla
  extract

40 g (1½ oz) unsalted butter

1 teaspoon coarse sea salt

400 g (14 oz) good-quality
  milk chocolate

sea salt flakes, to garnish
  (optional)

Lightly spray a 20 cm (8 inch) square cake tin with cooking oil spray. Line the tray with a long strip of baking paper, letting it overhang two sides, to make it easier to remove the caramel once it has set. Lightly spray the baking paper as well.

Put the sugar, glucose and golden syrup in a saucepan. Add 2 tablespoons water and stir, with a metal spoon, over high heat until the sugar has dissolved. Run a wet pastry brush around the inside edge of the pan to ensure there are no sugar crystals stuck to the side. Bring to the boil and cook until the temperature reaches 180°C (356°F) on a sugar thermometer.

Meanwhile, bring the cream to a simmer and add the vanilla. Remove from the heat and keep warm.

When the sugar mixture is at the right temperature, remove from the heat and use a metal spoon to stir in the warm cream mixture — this will arrest the cooking process and the temperature will drop.

Place the pan back over medium–high heat and stir regularly until the mixture reaches 127°C (260°F) on the sugar thermometer. Be very careful here as you don't want the mixture to burn — if you leave it alone, without stirring for too long, it will! At the same time, it shouldn't be constantly stirred. When it reaches the right temperature, immediately beat in the butter and salt until smooth.

Pour the mixture into the cake tin, tilting the tin slightly if it doesn't flow straight out to the edges. Leave to cool slightly, then refrigerate, uncovered, for 1½–2 hours, or until the caramel is firm, but not so hard that you can't cut through it. If you do end up leaving it longer, you'll need to sit the caramel at room temperature until it is soft enough to cut through.

Use the paper overhang to help you lift the caramel out of the tin, onto a chopping board. Dip a heavy, sharp knife in boiling water, then quickly but carefully dry it off and cut the caramel into 2 cm (¾ inch) squares. Place in a single layer on a baking tray lined with baking paper, neatly but not so they are touching. Refrigerate for another couple of hours, or until very firm.

Melt the chocolate in a heatproof bowl set over a saucepan of simmering water, ensuring the base of the bowl doesn't touch the water. Stir occasionally with a metal spoon until almost completely melted, then remove from the heat and continue to stir until very smooth and liquid.

Using a candy-dipping fork, or just a regular fork, dip each caramel square into the melted chocolate, allowing any excess to drip back into the bowl. Place on a tray lined with baking paper, keeping them slightly separated. Sprinkle the top with a few sea salt flakes if using. Refrigerate for about 1 hour, until set.

Store in an airtight container in single layers, separated by baking paper. In warm climates, keep the cobbers in the fridge, bringing them out of the fridge a few minutes before you serve them so they are not too hard to chew. They will keep in the fridge for several months.

Real fruit jubes

Fruit jellies, jubes, gels and gummies are all variations on a theme of gelatine-based confectionery. Of course, gummy lollies are not always fruit based — think black cats, witchetty grubs, milk bottles... or another of my favourites, wine gums. The jubes below are preservative free and use natural colours and flavours. Experiment with your favourite juice — citrus, apple, pear, cherry, berries, pomegranate, pineapple, grape, cranberry... And a mix of different flavours makes a killer party lolly bag!

Makes about 100 jubes

1 litre (35 fl oz/4 cups) strained fresh or bottled fruit juice of your choice (see Note)

220 g (7¾ oz/1 cup) caster (superfine) sugar, or to taste (see Note)

250 ml (9 fl oz/1 cup) liquid glucose

85 g (3 oz/½ cup) powdered gelatine (see Note)

170 ml (5½ fl oz/⅔ cup) boiling water

mild-flavoured cooking oil spray

220 g (7¾ oz/1 cup) granulated sugar, for coating

In a saucepan, heat the fruit juice, caster sugar and liquid glucose over high heat until the sugar has dissolved. Now bring to the boil, without stirring, and continue to boil until the mixture reaches 120°C (248°F) on a sugar thermometer. Remove from the heat.

Meanwhile, put the gelatine in a saucepan, then whisk in the boiling water until smooth. Place over low heat and stir with a metal spoon until the gelatine has completely dissolved.

Pour the gelatine mixture into the juice mixture and combine well.

Pour into a 20 cm (8 inch) square cake tin that has been sprayed with cooking oil spray. Cover the top of the tin with plastic wrap and store in a cool, dry place overnight. In warm weather, you can refrigerate it for a few hours, until solid.

When the jelly has set, pour most of the granulated sugar into a tray that has a lip around the edge. Sprinkle the remaining sugar onto your workbench. Briefly dip the base of the cake tin in hot water, then turn out onto the sugar-coated bench. Cut into 2 cm (¾ inch) squares, then roll them over the sugar-coated tray to evenly coat.

Store layered between sheets of baking paper in an airtight container in the fridge. They are best eaten within a few days, but will keep for up to 1 week.

Jubey jewels

Wine gums

Instead of fruit juice, use 750 ml (26 fl oz/3 cups) red or white wine, 2 tablespoons strained lemon or orange juice, 220 g (7¾ oz/1 cup) sugar and 250 ml (9 fl oz/1 cup) liquid glucose. Heat as instructed in the first step, then follow the rest of the recipe, dissolving the same quantity of gelatine in the same amount of boiling water, and setting, slicing, coating and storing as before.

Turn this into a **mulled wine gum** by adding spices such as a cinnamon stick, a good pinch of freshly grated nutmeg and a few whole cloves to the mix as you are heating; strain before adding the dissolved gelatine.

NOTE *The amount of sugar you need may change, depending on whether you are using fresh or bottled juice, the natural sweetness of fresh fruit and personal taste — you do need to use at least the amount stated in the recipe to get the consistency right, but it is okay to add a little bit more sugar if it needs it.*

If using bottled juice, no-added-sugar versions are best. If using fresh pineapple juice or kiwi fruit juice, you may need to add a little more gelatine, as both fruits contain a natural enzyme that can break down protein. Bottled pineapple juice will likely be already heat treated, so it's fine to follow the recipe as is.

Vienna almonds

All dressed up

Chocolate-dipped

After the nuts have cooled completely, tip them into a pan of melted chocolate (I use half dark, half milk chocolate) and stir with a metal spoon or silicon spatula until coated. Using a fork, individually transfer each almond to a tray lined with baking paper, allowing the excess chocolate to drip back into the pan, and spacing the almonds apart so they don't stick together.

Cinnamon sprinkle

Stir in a little ground cinnamon when you add the vanilla and salt in the second coating.

I've been addicted to Vienna almonds — a fancy name for toasted, caramelised almonds — ever since my mum first bought a packet from a nut shop in Sydney's Strand Arcade. When I discovered the dark chocolate-coated variety, an unhealthy dependency developed, and choosing between the two was challenging. Then there was the cinnamon variety to contend with… I still pop into that ornate arcade from time to time, mainly for the nostalgia of it all — but these are so easy to make that I don't feel so bad if it's a long time between city visits.

This simple recipe is also great for those sugared peanuts you can still sometimes buy — only without the red food colouring, which I'm loathe to add to anything these days.

Makes about 1½ cups

165 g (5¾ oz/¾ cup) caster (superfine) sugar

160 g (5½ oz/1 cup) whole almonds (blanched or skin on), toasted

½ teaspoon pure vanilla extract

a pinch of fine sea salt

Line a baking tray with baking paper and set aside.

Put 110 g (3¾ oz/½ cup) of the sugar in a saucepan with 1 tablespoon water. Stir constantly with a metal spoon over medium–high heat until the sugar has dissolved, then allow to come to the boil. Add the almonds, vanilla and salt and stir continuously for a few minutes, until the mixture looks a little like wet, pale sand and is coating the nuts.

Immediately tip the mixture onto your baking tray, using the metal spoon to lightly separate any large clumps of nuts. Allow to cool completely (which can take about 30 minutes, depending on the weather), then separate into individual nuts. They will have a whitish, uneven crust from the sugar.

Put the remaining sugar in a clean saucepan with 2 teaspoons water. Stir over medium–high heat until the sugar has dissolved. Allow to come to the boil, then cook, swirling the pan occasionally without stirring, until the mixture is an even amber colour and starts to smell like toffee.

Remove from the heat, add the separated almonds, very quickly toss together and tip out onto the lined baking tray again. The idea is not to cover the nuts completely, just to give them a bit of a toffee glaze over the top of the textured vanilla sugar. You do not want the crystallised sugar that coats the almonds in the first stages to dissolve into the toffee, which is why you need to work quickly. Again, separate the almonds gently with a spoon if there are any large clumps. Allow to cool completely, which could take up to an hour, then separate into individual almonds.

Store in an airtight container, in the fridge if the weather is humid, otherwise the pantry will be fine. The almonds will keep for up to 1 month… although there's no way they'd last that long in my house!

Contraband mints

When I was six or seven I boldly nicked some peppermint-filled chocolate from the local supermarket, because I was so addicted to the flavour. I secretly nibbled on it day and night, and went out of my way to hide the wrapper once I'd gobbled the entire thing. Turns out my dad had stolen a box of choc peppermint creams at a similar age, gorging on them until he was ill, so the inclination to illegally acquire mint chocolate is clearly hereditary. I still occasionally get smacked with a tidal wave of minty craving!

Makes 24–30 patties

330 g (11¾ oz/2¾ cups) icing sugar mixture

¼ teaspoon cream of tartar

1½ tablespoons liquid glucose

1 teaspoon peppermint extract

100 g (3½ oz) 70% dark chocolate, chopped

100 g (3½ oz) good-quality milk chocolate, chopped

25 g (1 oz) Copha (white vegetable shortening) or solid coconut oil

Place the icing sugar, cream of tartar, glucose and peppermint extract in the bowl of an electric mixer. Add 1½ tablespoons water and mix on low speed until the ingredients starts to come together, then beat on medium–high speed for a few minutes, or until you have a firm but pliable paste. (You can also mix the ingredients by hand, then knead for 5 minutes or so, until they come together into a pliable paste.)

Roll the paste out between two sheets of baking paper, to a thickness of 5 mm (¼ inch). Use a 3–4 cm (1¼–1½ inch) cookie cutter to stamp out discs (or other shapes). Place on a tray lined with baking paper, then refrigerate for 24 hours to dry them out a little and let the flavour and texture settle.

Before coating the mint patties in chocolate, place in the freezer for 1 hour.

Melt the dark chocolate, milk chocolate and Copha in a heatproof bowl set over a saucepan of simmering water, ensuring the base of the bowl doesn't touch the water. Stir occasionally with a metal spoon until almost completely melted, then remove from the heat and continue to stir until

very smooth and liquid. The chocolate should be no warmer than body temperature when you dip the patties into it.

One at a time, dip the patties into the chocolate, using a fork to lift them out, and allowing any excess chocolate to drip back into the bowl. Carefully slide onto another tray lined with baking paper. If the chocolate sets too much from the frozen patties, gently remelt and continue.

Refrigerate the chocolate-coated patties for several hours, or until the chocolate has completely set.

Store in single layers, between sheets of baking paper, in an airtight container in the fridge. These confectioneries will actually mellow and taste better a day or two after making them — if you can wait that long. They will last about 1 month in the fridge.

MINT DOESN'T GRAB YOU?
Instead of peppermint extract, try adding pure vanilla extract, musk essence, rosewater, orange blossom water or strong espresso coffee.

Crystallised ginger

Nana Doris kept a steady supply of crystallised ginger in a Chinese blue and white ceramic ginger jar that had long been emptied of its original contents. We'd dip into it from time to time, but no one else in the family really understood my grandmother's fascination for it; it seems my palate has now aligned itself with hers. I store some in the cupboard for nibbling on with a handful of nuts and dark chocolate, or adding to my Anzac biscuits, carrot cake, and even my Christmas fruit mince.

Makes about 1⅔ cups

2 large ginger roots (see Note), about 450 g (1 lb) in total

440 g (15½ oz/2 cups) caster (superfine) sugar, or raw caster (superfine) sugar

Peel the ginger, then cut the flesh into pieces roughly 1 cm x 2 cm (½ inch x ¾ inch) in size.

Place the ginger in a saucepan with 1.5 litres (52 fl oz/ 6 cups) water. Bring to the boil over high heat, then reduce to a steady simmer. Cover and cook for 3 hours, or until the ginger is starting to become tender.

Remove the lid. Stir in 385 g (13½ oz/1¾ cups) of the sugar until it dissolves, then cook, uncovered, for a further 3 hours, or until the ginger is quite tender when pierced with the tip of a sharp knife.

Line a baking tray with baking paper and sprinkle with the remaining sugar.

Using a slotted spoon, lift the ginger from the syrup, shaking off any excess syrup, then transfer to the sugared tray; reserve the syrup for other uses (see note). Turn the ginger to coat in the sugar, then spread the pieces out to dry; this should take a few hours, but will depend on the humidity.

Pop into an airtight jar or container just large enough to hold the ginger. The ginger will keep in your pantry for several months, but in very humid conditions is best kept in the fridge.

> **NOTE** *Young, shiny-skinned ginger may require a shorter cooking time than given in the recipe, and will be more tender and less fibrous than older ginger, which also has more 'heat'. The syrup can be used in hot drinks as a sweetener, but unlike the Ginger syrup on page 220 it will set hard, so you'll need to chip it off into pieces and melt these in boiling water. Add a splash of lemon juice for sore throats!*

Turkish delight

When I was around eight, my father's family used to play tennis on sunny Sunday afternoons. If my cousin Julie and I got bored, they'd send us off to the corner shop where we'd spend our pocket money on boxes of Turkish delight, which I'd eat until I felt queasy and reeked of roses or mint — the extent of their selection.

Many recipes these days call for gelatine, although starch as a thickener is more authentic, and vegetarian friendly. The result is lush, like a kiss. This recipe makes a big batch — after all, if you're going to stir the mixture for an hour, it has to be worth your while.

Extra delights

Coconut delight

Instead of the icing sugar mixture, use desiccated coconut to coat the Turkish delight.

Peppermint delight

Instead of rosewater, use 1–2 teaspoons peppermint extract, and green food colouring.

Makes 50 pieces

mild-flavoured cooking oil spray

1.3 kg (3 lb/6 cups) caster (superfine) sugar

2 tablespoons strained fresh lemon juice

185 g (6½ oz/1½ cups) cornflour (cornstarch)

2 scant teaspoons cream of tartar

2½ tablespoons rosewater

½ teaspoon pure vanilla extract

4 drops of red or pink food colouring (optional)

For dusting

375 g (13 oz/3 cups) icing (confectioners') sugar

185 g (6½ oz/1½ cups) cornflour (cornstarch)

Lightly spray a 20 x 30 cm (8 x 12 inch) slab tin with cooking oil spray. Line with a long strip of baking paper, letting it overhang two sides, to make it easier to remove the Turkish delight once it has set. Lightly spray the baking paper too.

Put the sugar and lemon juice in a saucepan with 500 ml (17 fl oz/2 cups) water. Stir with a metal spoon over high heat until the sugar has dissolved. Bring to the boil, stirring occasionally, until the syrup reaches 125°C (257°F) on a sugar thermometer. Turn off the heat.

Meanwhile, put the cornflour and cream of tartar in a saucepan, pour in 500 ml (17 fl oz/2 cups) water and whisk until smooth. Place over medium–high heat, whisking until the mixture boils and becomes a sticky, gel-like mixture. Keep whisking regularly for 4–5 minutes, or until the mixture turns into a white, cloudy paste. Remove from the heat.

Add 60 ml (2 fl oz/¼ cup) of the sugar syrup at a time to the paste, whisking well between each addition; as the mixture becomes smooth and more fluid, you can add the rest of the syrup more quickly. Place back over medium–high heat and bring the mixture just to the boil as you stir.

Reduce the heat to a simmer and cook for 45–50 minutes, stirring frequently, until the mixture becomes a golden colour. Add the rosewater, vanilla and food colouring, if using, and stir until well combined and evenly coloured.

Pour into your slab tin, gently shaking the tin to allow the mixture to settle evenly. Leave to set overnight — do not cover or put in the fridge.

The next day, combine the icing sugar and cornflour in a bowl and liberally sift about 125 g (4½ oz/1 cup) of the mixture over a 25 x 35 cm (10 x 14 inch) patch of workbench directly in front of you.

Lift the Turkish delight out of the tin and invert onto the dusted surface. Remove the baking paper and liberally sprinkle more of the mixture over the top.

Spray a sharp knife with cooking oil spray, then cut the Turkish delight into 3 cm x 4 cm (1¼ inch x 1½ inch) pieces. Roll each piece in the remaining icing sugar mixture.

Pack the Turkish delight squares in single layers between sheets of baking paper, liberally sprinkling each layer with more icing sugar mixture to stop them sticking together. Store them in an airtight container in a cool dark place, or in the fridge.

The Turkish delight will last for a few months, although after a while the sugar will start to break down and soften.

Chapter 4

PIE SHOP

THE ICONIC MEAT pie was one of my first strong food memories, and will likely be the most enduring. Back at school, an encounter with the phrase 'meat pie with dead horse' — rhyming slang for 'sauce' — fascinated me so much that I purchased a badge featuring a pie with horse-shaped sauce. Today the phrase could just as well be referring to the filling, rather than the blood-red sauce… so the best way to know exactly what is in your pie is to make it yourself!

Save yourself time, energy and money by doubling the recipes and freezing the unbaked pies. Simply pop a couple in the oven when the pie craving arrives (usually on a cold, drizzly day for me). And if you're baking for a crowd, do be sure to put a little pastry decoration — a chook's head, a cross, a heart, or sesame/poppy seeds — on your pie lids, so you know what is in each.

Aussie beef pies

This is the quintessential Australian beef pie, flavoured with beer and Vegemite. You'll notice I've given two options for the meat filling. If you like your pies a little chunky and more rustic, use chuck steak; if you prefer them more like the ones you get at the footy, use minced beef. Use this recipe as a base for the variations on pages 152–153.

Makes 6 individual pies

2 tablespoons olive oil

1½ tablespoons butter

1 brown onion, finely chopped

2 tablespoons plain (all-purpose) flour, plus extra for dusting

600 g (1 lb 5 oz) chuck steak, cut into 2 cm (¾ inch) dice — or 650 g (1 lb 7 oz) minced (ground) beef

250 ml (9 fl oz/1 cup) beer

375 ml (13 fl oz/1½ cups) beef stock

1 small carrot, finely diced

1 celery stalk, finely diced

2 garlic cloves, crushed

½ teaspoon finely chopped fresh thyme

1 tablespoon tomato paste (concentrated purée)

1½ tablespoons worcestershire sauce

1½ teaspoons Vegemite (or Promite or Marmite if unavailable)

1 fresh bay leaf

1 quantity of Savoury shortcrust pastry (page 224), or 3 sheets ready-rolled frozen pastry, thawed

½ quantity of Puff pastry (page 225), or 3 sheets ready-rolled frozen pastry, thawed

1 egg, lightly beaten

Tomato sauce (page 226), to serve

To make the filling, put half the olive oil and half the butter in a saucepan over medium–high heat and sauté the onion for 10 minutes, or until lightly golden. Remove from the pan and set aside.

If using chuck steak, season the flour well with sea salt and freshly cracked black pepper, then toss together with the beef cubes until they are lightly coated. Add the remaining oil and butter to the pan, then sauté the beef over high heat in several batches until lightly golden, adding a little more oil if needed. Set aside with the onion.

If using minced beef, brown it in batches in the remaining oil, but reserve the remaining butter. Add the butter to the pan once the mince has been browned and removed, then stir in the flour and cook for a minute or so.

Add the beer and stock to the pan, scraping up any cooked-on bits. Return the beef and onion to the pan, along with the carrot, celery, garlic, thyme, tomato paste, worcestershire sauce, Vegemite and bay leaf. Bring to the boil, then reduce the heat and simmer for 1¼ hours, or until the beef is very tender and the sauce is thick and rich. Discard the bay leaf, then season to taste.

Cool the mixture slightly, then cover and refrigerate for 4 hours, or until completely cold; if you can leave it overnight, the flavours will develop even more.

To assemble and bake the pies

Remove the shortcrust pastry from the fridge 15 minutes (a little less or more on a hot or cold day) to soften slightly before you roll it out; it should still be cold.

Using a fine sieve, very lightly flour your work surface and a rolling pin. Starting at the middle of the shortcrust pastry disc, gently roll the pastry away from you, then turn it 45 degrees and roll away from you again. Repeat this process until the pastry is a uniform 2 mm (¹⁄₁₆ inch) thickness. Use a 15 cm (6 inch) round pastry cutter to cut six shortcrust pastry discs for the pie bases.

Lightly grease six individual, non-stick pie tins, measuring about 12 cm (4½ inches) across the top, 8 cm (3¼ inches) across the base and 3.5 cm (1½ inches) deep.

Line each pie tin with a shortcrust pastry round, gently pressing the dough into the tins, starting in the centre and working out towards the top rim of the tins; stop when the pastry is about 1 cm (¾ inch) above the line of the tin. Gently fold this bit of pastry down over to line the pie tin rims — this is where the pie pastry lids will adhere. Place the pie tins on a baking tray, lightly cover with a sheet of plastic wrap and refrigerate for 2 hours.

About 15 minutes before you're ready to resume making the pies, take the puff pastry out of the fridge to soften slightly, making sure it is still cold.

Divide the cold filling among the pie bases. Roll the puff pastry out to a 5 mm (½ inch) thickness and cut out six 12.5 cm (5 inch) rounds. Lightly brush the rims of the shortcrust pastry with the beaten egg. Top each pie with a puff pastry round, pressing down around the edges to help the two different pastries adhere to each other; you can pinch the edges together if you really want to be sure, or use the back of a fork to seal around the edge. Pierce the top of each pie with a small sharp knife or skewer to form an air vent, then brush the top of the pies with more beaten egg, avoiding the vent. Place the pies back in the fridge for 30 minutes before baking — this will give the lids of the pies more puff and crispness.

Put two baking trays in the oven and preheat the oven to 200°C (400°F).

Place the pie tins directly onto the hot baking trays and bake for 10 minutes, or until the pastry is puffed and lightly golden. Turn the oven temperature down to 180°C (350°F) and bake the pies for a further 10–15 minutes to ensure the filling is hot — your pastry should have a pretty good tan by now!

Remove the pies from the oven and the tins. Serve hot, with tomato sauce.

Hearty lamb & rosemary pies

Aussies produce good lamb, so it just wouldn't be proper not to include a lamb pie in this chapter. The really good news is that more economical slow-cooked cuts make for particularly delectable fillings. Try inventing your own pie, using your favourite lamb stew or curry — you know you have one. Or your mum does.

Makes 6 individual pies

2 tablespoons olive oil

1½ tablespoons butter

1 brown onion, finely chopped

2 tablespoons plain (all-purpose) flour

600 g (1 lb 5 oz) lamb shoulder, or the meat from forequarter chops, cut into 2 cm (¾ inch) dice

125 ml (4 fl oz/½ cup) white wine

500 ml (17 fl oz/2 cups) rich chicken stock

1 carrot, cut into 1 cm (½ inch) dice

1 celery stalk, cut into 1 cm (½ inch) dice

150 g (5½ oz) turnip, swede (rutabaga) or parsnip, or a combination, peeled and cut into 1 cm (½ inch) dice

3 garlic cloves, crushed

½ teaspoon finely chopped fresh rosemary

¼ teaspoon finely grated lemon zest

2 teaspoons worcestershire sauce

1 fresh bay leaf

1 quantity of Savoury shortcrust pastry (page 224), or 3 sheets ready-rolled frozen pastry, thawed

½ quantity of Puff pastry (page 225), or 3 sheets ready-rolled frozen pastry, thawed

1 egg, lightly beaten

Tomato sauce (page 226), to serve (optional)

To make the filling, put half the olive oil and half the butter in a saucepan over medium–high heat and sauté the onion for 10 minutes, or until lightly golden. Remove from the pan and set aside.

Season the flour with sea salt and freshly cracked black pepper, then toss together with the lamb cubes until they are lightly coated. Add the remaining oil and butter to the saucepan, then sauté the lamb over high heat in several batches until lightly golden, adding a little more oil if needed. Set aside with the onion.

Add the wine and stock to the pan, scraping up any cooked-on bits. Return the lamb and onion to the pan, along with the carrot, celery, turnip, garlic, rosemary, lemon zest, worcestershire sauce and bay leaf. Bring to the boil, then reduce the heat and simmer for 1½ hours, or until the lamb is very tender and the sauce is thick and rich. Discard the bay leaf, then season to taste.

Cool the mixture slightly, then cover and refrigerate for 4 hours, or until completely cold; if you can leave it overnight, the flavours will develop even more.

To assemble and bake the pies, see the instructions for the Aussie beef pies on page 150.

Serve hot, with tomato sauce if desired.

'Roast lamb dinner with mint sauce' pie

Replace 2 tablespoons of the wine with white wine vinegar, and the rosemary with 1 tablespoon finely chopped mint. Omit the lemon zest. Replace the turnip, swede or parsnip with equal amounts of diced potato and pumpkin (winter squash). Add 40 g (1½ oz/¼ cup) cooked peas and another 1 teaspoon finely chopped mint to the chilled mixture before filling the pies.

More beefy BEAUTIES

Still hungry for meat pies? Try these scrumptious variations, using the Aussie beef pies recipe on pages 148–150 as your guide.

Cheese & bacon

When sautéing the onion, add 2 finely chopped streaky bacon rashers. Omit the Vegemite. Cut 60 g (2¼ oz) cheddar or edam cheese into small dice and divide over the cold filling just after you fill the pies, and before putting the lids on. Gently poke the cheese down into the mix, so it isn't a molten lava eruption when you bite into the pies.

Steak & mushroom

Use chuck steak, not minced (ground) beef. Add 125 g (4½ oz) finely sliced flat or button mushrooms to the saucepan with the other vegetables. Drop the beer back to 185 ml (6 fl oz/¾ cup).

Beef burgundy

Use chuck steak, not minced (ground) beef. When sautéing the onion, add 1 finely chopped streaky bacon rasher. Replace the beer with red wine, and decrease the stock by 2 tablespoons. Increase the thyme by ½ teaspoon, and drop the Vegemite back to ½ teaspoon. Add 100 g (3½ oz) sliced button mushrooms when adding the vegetables to the saucepan.

Steak diane

Use chuck steak, not minced (ground) beef. Replace the beer with 60 ml (2 fl oz/¼ cup) brandy and 125 ml (4 fl oz/½ cup) thin (pouring) cream. Increase the stock by 60 ml (2 fl oz/ ¼ cup), and use 3 garlic cloves. Omit the tomato paste and Vegemite, and instead add 1 tablespoon dijon mustard and 2 teaspoons lemon juice. Stir 2 tablespoons finely chopped flat-leaf (Italian) parsley and a good grind of black pepper through the chilled filling before dividing it among the pastry bases.

Potato-topped

Omit the puff pastry lids. Instead, cook 1 kg (2 lb 4 oz) floury potatoes in their skins until very tender. Peel while still hot, then mash the potatoes with 1½ tablespoons butter, 60 ml (2 fl oz/¼ cup) thin (pouring) cream and 2 teaspoons sea salt until smooth. You can add a little bit more butter or cream if you like, but make sure the mixture is still thick enough to pipe and hold its shape. Fill a piping (icing) bag fitted with a star-shaped nozzle. Starting at the centre of the pie filling, pipe in a circular motion to form a single layer of potato over the pie filling, before the pies go into the oven to bake. Potato tops can replace the puff pastry in any of the savoury pie recipes in this book.

Curried beef

Replace the beer with 250 ml (9 fl oz/1 cup) coconut milk. Add 1½–2 tablespoons of your favourite curry powder or paste when you add the vegetables to the saucepan. Replace the thyme with 2 teaspoons chopped coriander (cilantro) root and 1 tablespoon chopped coriander leaves. Drop the worcestershire sauce back to 1 tablespoon. Omit the Vegemite.

Creamy chicken, leek & mushroom pies

I might be an Aussie lass, but I was born with a love of rich, cream-based sauces coursing through my veins. If you happen to have a copy of my *Snowflakes and Schnapps* cookbook, which is full of rich, cold-weather recipes, you'll already be aware of my Germanic/Scandi heritage. I adore a really good creamy chicken pie, and will choose it over the traditional meat pie any day. Handing in my citizenship...

Makes 6 individual pies

2 tablespoons olive oil

2 tablespoons butter

1 large leek, white part only, finely sliced

6 small Swiss brown mushrooms, sliced

3 tablespoons plain (all-purpose) flour

600 g (1 lb 5 oz) skinless chicken thigh fillets, cut into 2 cm (¾ inch) dice

80 ml (2½ fl oz/⅓ cup) white wine

250 ml (9 fl oz/1 cup) rich chicken stock

185 ml (6 fl oz/¾ cup) thin (pouring) cream

½ teaspoon freshly grated nutmeg

1 small carrot, cut into 1 cm (½ inch) dice

1 long celery stalk, cut into 1 cm (½ inch) dice

3 garlic cloves, crushed

1½ teaspoons finely chopped fresh thyme or tarragon

¼ teaspoon finely grated lemon zest (optional)

1 tablespoon dijon mustard

1 fresh bay leaf

1 quantity of Savoury shortcrust pastry (page 224), or 3 sheets ready-rolled frozen pastry, thawed

½ quantity of Puff pastry (page 225), or 3 sheets ready-rolled frozen pastry, thawed

To make the filling, put half the olive oil and 2 teaspoons of the butter in a saucepan over medium–high heat and sauté the leek for 10 minutes, or until softened and very lightly golden. Remove from the pan and set aside.

Add another 2 teaspoons of butter to the pan and sauté the mushrooms with a large pinch of sea salt for 3 minutes, or until the mushrooms are soft and there is no liquid left in the pan. Remove from the pan and set aside with the leek.

Season the flour well with sea salt and freshly cracked black pepper, then toss together with the chicken pieces until they are lightly coated. Add the remaining oil and butter to the saucepan and sauté the chicken over high heat in several batches until lightly golden, adding a little more oil if needed. Set aside with the leek and mushroom.

Add the wine, stock and cream to the pan, scraping up any cooked-on bits. Return the chicken, leek and mushrooms to the pan, along with the nutmeg, carrot, celery, garlic, thyme, lemon zest, mustard and bay leaf. Bring to the boil, then reduce the heat and simmer for 1 hour, or until the chicken is very tender and the sauce is thick and rich. Discard the bay leaf, then season to taste.

Cool the mixture slightly, then cover and refrigerate for 4 hours, or until completely cold; if you can leave it overnight, the flavours will develop even more.

To assemble and bake the pies, see the instructions for the Aussie beef pies on page 150.

Serve hot.

More chicken classics

Coq au vin

Replace the Swiss brown mushrooms with 6 quartered button mushrooms; add them to the pan when sautéing the leek, along with 1 finely chopped streaky bacon rasher. Instead of the white wine, use 185 ml (6 fl oz/¾ cup) red wine. Omit the cream and add 125 ml (4 fl oz/½ cup) tomato passata. Use 4 garlic cloves, and choose thyme as your herb. Omit the lemon zest.

Mexicana

When sautéing the leek, add half a small finely chopped capsicum (pepper). Replace the wine with Mexican-style beer. When adding the stock and beer to the pan, also add 50 g (1¾ oz/¼ cup) corn kernels, 1 teaspoon ground cumin, 1 teaspoon spicy sweet smoked paprika and ½ teaspoon finely chopped fresh coriander (cilantro) root. Replace the cream with tomato purée. Use 4 garlic cloves, and 2 tablespoons finely chopped coriander (cilantro) as your herb, but only stir it through the mixture just before filling pies. Divide 20 g (¾ oz) grated cheddar cheese over the top of the filled pies before you top with the lids.

Curried chicken pie

Replace the white wine and cream with 310 ml (10¾ fl oz/1¼ cups) coconut milk. Replace the nutmeg with 1½ tablespoons of your favourite curry powder or paste. Replace 1½ tablespoons of the stock with lemon juice. Use 4 garlic cloves, and add 2 teaspoons finely grated fresh ginger with the garlic. Replace the herbs with 2 teaspoons finely chopped coriander (cilantro) root. When the mixture is chilled, stir in 1 tablespoon finely chopped coriander leaves before filling the pies. If using a Thai curry paste, you can add 1–2 fresh kaffir lime leaves to the pan as the curry is simmering and remove them, with the bay leaf, before filling the pies.

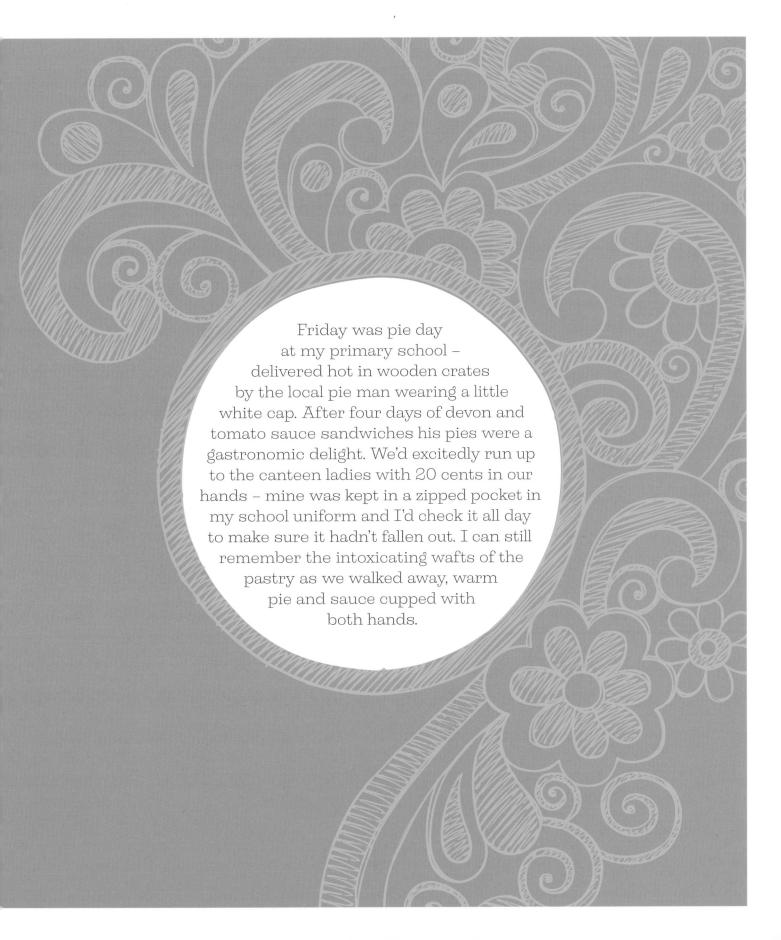

Friday was pie day
at my primary school –
delivered hot in wooden crates
by the local pie man wearing a little
white cap. After four days of devon and
tomato sauce sandwiches his pies were a
gastronomic delight. We'd excitedly run up
to the canteen ladies with 20 cents in our
hands – mine was kept in a zipped pocket in
my school uniform and I'd check it all day
to make sure it hadn't fallen out. I can still
remember the intoxicating wafts of the
pastry as we walked away, warm
pie and sauce cupped with
both hands.

Cauliflower cheese pies

I'd planned to develop something beyond your average vegie pie, and this seems to have hit the mark. My helpful meat-eating taste testers said they'd 'go that' any day! It is more rich and flavoursome than you'd imagine, and if you omit the pastry you're left with an excellent vegie bake with savoury crumble topping.

Makes 6 individual pies

1 small cauliflower, broken into 4 cm (1½ inch) florets

60 ml (2 fl oz/¼ cup) olive oil

½ teaspoon ground cumin

½ teaspoon ground sweet paprika or smoked sweet paprika

500 ml (17 fl oz/2 cups) full-cream milk

2 fresh bay leaves

2½ tablespoons butter

1 large brown onion, finely chopped

35 g (1¼ oz/¼ cup) plain (all-purpose) flour

¼ teaspoon freshly grated nutmeg

100 g (3½ oz/1 cup) grated cheddar cheese

1 large garlic clove, very finely chopped

2 spring onions (scallions), green part only, chopped

ground white pepper, to taste

1 quantity of Savoury shortcrust pastry (page 224), or 3 sheets ready-rolled frozen pastry, thawed

Almond & herb crumble topping

120 g (4¼ oz) cold butter, cut into 1.5 cm (⅝ inch) cubes

5 tablespoons plain (all-purpose) flour

70 g (2½ oz/⅔ cup) ground almonds

70 g (2½ oz/⅔ cup) finely grated parmesan

½ teaspoon very finely grated, then chopped, lemon zest

1 tablespoon finely chopped flat-leaf (Italian) parsley

Preheat the oven to 200°C (400°F). Toss the cauliflower florets with the olive oil, cumin and paprika and season well with sea salt. Spread them in a roasting tin and roast for 40 minutes to 1 hour, or until the cauliflower is very tender, golden brown and crusty on the edges. Drain on paper towel and cool.

Meanwhile, in a small saucepan, bring the milk and bay leaves to a simmer. Turn off the heat, but leave the pan on the element to let the milk infuse and keep it warm.

In another saucepan, melt 1 tablespoon of the butter and gently sauté the onion over medium heat for about 5 minutes, or until softened; don't allow to colour. Remove from the pan and set aside.

Melt the remaining butter in the pan over medium heat. Add the flour and cook, stirring, for 1 minute. Remove the bay leaves from the warm milk mixture, then stir it into the roux with the nutmeg until smooth. Cook for 5 minutes, or until the sauce has thickened considerably. Remove from the heat, then stir in the cheese, garlic and spring onion greens. Add the cauliflower and sautéed onion and gently but thoroughly combine. Season to taste with sea salt and ground white pepper. Cover and chill for 2 hours.

When ready to bake the pies, line six individual pie tins with shortcrust pastry as instructed on page 150. Chill for 10 minutes.

Put two baking trays in the oven and preheat to 200°C (400°F). Meanwhile, put all the crumble topping ingredients into the bowl of a food processor and pulse until the mixture clumps together.

Divide the cauliflower filling among the pie bases. Divide the crumble mixture over the top. Place the pie tins directly onto the hot baking trays and bake for 10 minutes to give your base crust a good boost of heat.

Turn the oven temperature down to 180°C (350°F) and bake the pies for a further 10–15 minutes, to ensure the filling is hot. If the topping is browning too quickly, lay some foil over the top, with the shiny side up.

Remove the pies from the oven and the tins. Serve hot.

Quiche

'Real men don't eat quiche'? Good: more for me. There is something so satisfying about a simple quiche, just as long as the proportions and cooking times are spot on! Silken, savoury custard dotted with flavoursome ingredients encased in a buttery pastry shell is one heck of a comfort food. Quiche makes a fabulous breakfast on the run, and holds its own served cold too, making it perfect for picnics. You'll find more lovely filling ideas over the page, but don't let these stop you inventing your ultimate eggy pie.

Makes 6 individual quiches

1 quantity of Savoury shortcrust pastry (page 224), or 3 sheets ready-rolled frozen pastry, thawed

1 tablespoon butter

1 large brown onion, finely chopped

3 streaky bacon rashers, finely chopped

½ teaspoon very finely chopped fresh thyme

100 g (3½ oz/1 cup) grated gruyère or cheddar cheese

3 large eggs, plus 4 large egg yolks

185 ml (6 fl oz/¾ cup) thin (pouring) cream

185 g (6½ oz/¾ cup) crème fraîche or sour cream

a couple of good pinches of freshly grated nutmeg

Lightly grease six individual, non-stick pie tins, measuring about 12 cm (4½ inches) across the top, 8 cm (3¼ inches) across the base and 3.5 cm (1½ inches) deep. Roll the pastry out to a uniform 2–3 mm (1/16–1/8 inch) thickness. With the tip of a sharp knife, cut out six 15 cm (6 inch) diameter rounds. (You may like to trace this size round onto some baking paper, cut it out with scissors, then use it as a template.)

Carefully press each pastry round into the bottom of a pie tin. Press around the edges to gently ease the pastry up above the edge of the tin by 1 cm (½ inch). Decorate by pinching around the top edge, if you like. Refrigerate for 30 minutes.

Preheat the oven to 190°C (375°F).

Place the quiche tins on two baking trays. Line each pastry shell with a square of baking paper and cover the base with pie weights, baking beads or uncooked rice. Blind-bake for 6–7 minutes, then remove the paper and weights and return the tins to the oven for a further 5 minutes, or until the pastry is pale golden and dry all over. Remove the baking trays from the oven and turn the oven temperature down to 160°C (315°F).

While the pastry shells are blind-baking, prepare the filling. Melt the butter in a frying pan over medium heat. Add the onion, bacon and thyme and cook for 6–8 minutes, or until the onion has softened and is lightly golden. Remove from the pan and allow to cool.

Divide the onion mixture among the pie tins and scatter the cheese over the top.

In a bowl with a pouring lip, whisk together the eggs, egg yolks, cream, crème fraîche and nutmeg until smooth, then lightly season with sea salt and freshly ground black pepper. Carefully pour into the pastry shells so that they are evenly filled; each will take about 80 ml (2½ fl oz/⅓ cup) of liquid.

Return the trays to the oven. Bake for 20–25 minutes, or until the egg is just set, but still a little wobbly. Carefully remove from the oven, but leave the tins on the trays for 10 minutes, to allow the custard to continue to set.

Remove the quiches from the tins and serve warm, perhaps with a salad, or cold in a picnic basket for those lazy summer afternoons under a huge shady tree.

NOTE You can also make this quiche in a large deep flan (tart) tin, 26 cm (10½ inches) diameter and 5–6 cm (2–2½ inches) deep. You will need to blind-bake the pastry for 12 minutes before removing the baking paper and pie weights, then cook for a further 6 minutes to dry the pastry out. After adding the filling, it will take about 40–45 minutes to cook the egg mixture. You can also omit the pastry and make a baked frittata instead. It will take less time to cook, so remember to keep an eye on it.

Eggsellent fillings!

Using the recipe on the previous page as your guide, you can easily make a whole range of quiches. Just note that you may have a teensy bit of egg mixture left over, depending on how much filling you add — don't go too crazy, or you won't have enough custard to hold the quiche together. You just want to flavour the quiche, not pack it like a pie.

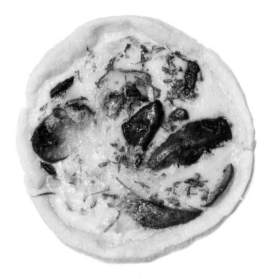

Spinach & goat's feta

Omit the bacon (optional), thyme and gruyère. When you sauté the onion, towards the end add 1 very finely chopped garlic clove and a few handfuls of baby English spinach leaves; sprinkle with ¼ teaspoon freshly grated nutmeg and sauté until the spinach has wilted. Leave to cool, then add to the blind-baked pastry shells. Divide 65 g (2¼ oz/ ½ cup) soft goat's feta cheese among the pastry shells. Mix ½ teaspoon very finely grated lemon zest through the egg mixture before pouring it over the spinach and cheese. You can also add 1 teaspoon finely chopped fresh mint or oregano with the egg or spinach if desired.

Mushroom & gruyère

Omit the bacon if desired. After you've sautéed the onion and thyme, remove the mixture from the pan. Add a few teaspoons of extra butter to the pan, with 2 crushed garlic cloves and 135 g (4¾ oz/1½ cups) finely sliced mushrooms of your choice. Sprinkle with salt and pepper and cook for 5 minutes, or until the mushrooms are starting to wilt. Add 1 tablespoon brandy and cook for a further 8–10 minutes, or until the mushrooms are tender and there is no liquid left in the pan. Combine the onion and mushrooms and divide among the blind-baked pastry shells. Add 1 tablespoon finely chopped flat-leaf (Italian) parsley and 1½ teaspoons dijon mustard, if desired, to the egg and cream mixture. Use gruyère instead of cheddar; also try using a mild, soft blue-vein cheese too.

Seafood

Omit the bacon and thyme. Instead of the onion, sauté the finely chopped white part of 1 large leek. Leave to cool, then add to the blind-baked pastry shells. Take 180 g (6½ oz) of one or more of the following: chopped raw prawns (shrimp), smoked salmon strips, diced raw salmon, chopped raw squid, small raw scallops or diced meaty scallops, or small oysters. Divide the seafood among the pastry shells; there should be 30 g (1 oz) in each. To the egg and cream mixture, add 1 tablespoon finely chopped fresh dill, 1 tablespoon finely chopped chives, 1½–2 teaspoons horseradish cream (optional) and ½ teaspoon finely grated lemon zest.

Chicken, asparagus & tarragon

Omit the thyme if desired. Divide 200 g (7 oz) cooked, diced chicken thighs (I just lightly poach mine in chicken stock) over the sautéed onion in the blind-baked pastry shells. Blanch 4–6 slender asparagus spears (in the leftover chicken stock), cut into 2 cm (¾ inch) lengths and divide among the pastry shells. To the egg and cream mixture, add ¼ teaspoon finely grated lemon zest, 1 teaspoon dijon mustard, 2 teaspoons white wine and 1 tablespoon chopped fresh tarragon. If tarragon isn't in season, use dill instead, or simply use thyme as in the original recipe.

Cornish pasties

Swede is the vegetable traditionally used in pasties, but it isn't always easy to find outside winter, in which case you can use carrot instead... even though to do so is apparently blasphemous! I've kept this recipe true to my childhood memories, but snuck in a splash of worcestershire sauce, which isn't traditional, so feel free to add some soft fresh herbs or spices of your own liking — just don't tell your Cornish cousins.

Makes 6 individual pasties

250 g (9 oz) skirt steak, cut into 1 cm (½ inch) dice

1 large waxy (boiling) or all-purpose potato, such as nicola, desiree or pontiac, cut into 8 mm (⅜ inch) dice

1 onion, finely chopped

70 g (2½ oz) swede (rutabaga) or carrot, cut into 8 mm (⅜ inch) dice

1 celery stalk, cut into 8 mm (⅜ inch) dice

1½ teaspoons worcestershire sauce

1 small egg

2 teaspoons milk or thin (pouring) cream

30 g (1 oz) butter

2 quantities of Savoury shortcrust pastry (page 224), or 6 sheets ready-rolled frozen shortcrust pastry, thawed

Preheat the oven to 170°C (325°F). Line two baking trays with baking paper.

In a bowl, combine the steak, potato, onion, swede, celery and worcestershire sauce. Season well with sea salt and freshly cracked black pepper.

In a small bowl, lightly whisk together the egg and milk until smooth; set aside.

Roll your pastry out to 2 mm (¹⁄₁₆ inch) thick, then cut out six 18 cm (7 inch) diameter rounds. Divide the meat and vegetable mixture among the pastry rounds, keeping it neatly in the centre. Top each with a teaspoon of butter. Lightly brush around the edge of one half of each pastry round with the egg wash, then fold over one side of the pastry to meet the other, forming a half-moon shape. Press down lightly, fold the pastry edge up and over itself, then pinch together all the way around — or you can use a fork to crimp the edges together if you find this a little easier.

Transfer the pasties to the baking trays. Using a sharp knife, pierce a small air vent in the top of each one, then brush with more egg wash.

Bake for 45–50 minutes, or until the pastry is deeply golden, and the beef and vegetables are cooked through and tender.

These pasties are best served immediately; if you are making them ahead of time you can gently reheat them in the oven before serving.

GOOD 'N' SAVOURY
Sausage rolls

Most sausage rolls throughout my life have been disappointingly cardboard-like, but in recent years they have been raised to the gourmet platform by a few clever bakers. Make sure you use marbled minced meat in the filling: don't go for that expensive, fat-free mince, as it will only dry out your filling. Also, keep an eye on your oven – they're all different – and don't let your rolls overcook, as that's a sure-fire way to suck them dry too. Which takes us back to cardboard.

Makes 12

1½ tablespoons olive oil

1 brown onion, very finely chopped

1 large celery stalk, very finely chopped

6 garlic cloves, crushed

1.2 kg (2 lb 10 oz) marbled minced (ground) pork

90 g (3¼ oz/1½ cups) breadcrumbs, made from two-day-old bread

1 tablespoon fine sea salt

1½ teaspoons ground white pepper

4 tablespoons finely chopped fresh sage leaves

¼ teaspoon ground celery seeds

1½ tablespoons ground fennel seeds

1 quantity of Puff pastry (page 225), or 3 sheets ready-rolled frozen puff pastry, thawed

1 egg

80 ml (2½ fl oz/⅓ cup) full-cream milk

Tomato sauce (page 226), to serve (optional)

Heat the olive oil in a frying pan over medium heat and sauté the onion, celery and garlic for 5 minutes, or until softened. Cool slightly, then add to a large bowl with the pork, breadcrumbs, salt, white pepper, sage, celery seeds and fennel seeds. Using very clean hands, mix together well. Really get in there and squish the mixture together for several minutes, to ensure it is very well combined.

Divide the mixture into six equal portions. Roll each portion into a log about 30 cm (12 inches) long and 3 cm (1¼ inches) in diameter. Place on a tray lined with baking paper, then cover and set aside in the refrigerator while you roll out your pastry.

To assemble and bake the rolls

Cut the pastry into six even strips. Keep one piece on your work surface and place the other pieces in the fridge to stay cool if your kitchen is hot.

Roll one pastry strip into a 15 x 30 cm (6 x 12 inch) rectangle. Place a log of filling in the centre of the pastry, running lengthways. Lightly beat together the egg and milk to form an egg wash. Brush this lightly down one edge of the pastry. Fold the pastry over the filling to meet the other pastry edge, then press together to tightly enclose the pastry. Leave the ends open. Cut the pastry log in half, to form two 15 cm (6 inch) long sausage rolls.

Place, seam side down, on a baking tray lined with baking paper. Brush the top lightly with egg wash. Place in the fridge while you repeat with the remaining pastry and filling, to make 12 sausage rolls in total.

Preheat the oven to 200°C (400°F). Bake the rolls for 30–35 minutes, or until they are golden brown and just cooked through. Serve hot, with tomato sauce if desired.

Lamb, spring onion & minted pea
Sausage rolls

In this variation on the recipe from the previous page, the addition of peas, mint and lemon to lamb results in a lighter, more elegant sausage roll – great in warmer months.

Makes 12

1½ tablespoons olive oil

10 spring onions (scallions), very finely sliced

115 g (4 oz/¾ cup) cooked peas

6 garlic cloves, crushed

20 g (¾ oz/⅓ cup) finely chopped fresh mint

1.2 kg (2 lb 10 oz) marbled minced (ground) lamb

60 g (2¼ oz/1 cup) breadcrumbs, made from two-day-old bread

1¼ teaspoons very finely chopped lemon zest

1½ teaspoons ground white pepper

1½ teaspoons freshly cracked black pepper

1 tablespoon sea salt

1 quantity of Puff pastry (page 225), or 3 sheets ready-rolled frozen puff pastry, thawed

1 egg

80 ml (2½ fl oz/⅓ cup) full-cream milk

Tomato sauce (page 226), to serve (optional)

Heat the olive oil in a frying pan over medium heat and sauté the spring onion for a few minutes, or until softened. Add the peas, garlic and mint and stir for 30 seconds, then remove from the heat. Cool slightly, then place in a large bowl with the lamb, breadcrumbs, lemon zest, peppers and salt. Using very clean hands, mix together well. Really get in there and squish the mixture together for several minutes, to ensure it is very well combined.

Divide the mixture into six equal portions, then roll each into a log about 30 cm (12 inches) long and 3 cm (1¼ inches) in diameter. Place on a tray lined with baking paper, then cover and set aside in the refrigerator while you roll out your pastry.

To roll out the pastry, and assemble and bake the rolls, follow the instructions for the Good 'n' savoury sausage rolls recipe on page 166.

Serve hot, with tomato sauce if desired.

Smoky beef, bacon & tomato Sausage rolls

Makes 12

Warm spices and smoky bacon pack these little rippers with the kind of winter flavours that will have you reaching for the red! And I don't mean tomato sauce.

1½ tablespoons olive oil

1 brown onion, very finely chopped

3 streaky bacon rashers, very finely chopped

1 carrot, very finely diced

1 celery stalk, very finely diced

6 garlic cloves, crushed

1½ teaspoons very finely chopped fresh thyme

1.2 kg (2 lb 10 oz) marbled minced (ground) beef

60 g (2¼ oz/1 cup) breadcrumbs, made from two-day-old bread

90 g (3¼ oz/⅓ cup) tomato paste (concentrated purée)

¼ teaspoon cayenne pepper (or more, if you love heat!)

1½ teaspoons smoked paprika

1½ teaspoons freshly cracked black pepper

2½ teaspoons ground cumin

2½ teaspoons ground cinnamon

1½ teaspoons ground coriander

2½ teaspoons sea salt

1 quantity of Puff pastry (page 225), or 3 sheets ready-rolled frozen puff pastry, thawed

1 egg

80 ml (2½ fl oz/⅓ cup) full-cream milk

Tomato sauce (page 226), to serve (optional)

Heat the olive oil in a frying pan over medium heat and sauté the onion, bacon, carrot and celery for 6 minutes, or until the vegetables have softened. Add the garlic and thyme and stir for 30 seconds, then remove from the heat. Cool slightly, then place in a large bowl with the beef, breadcrumbs, tomato paste, spices and salt. Using very clean hands, mix together well. Really get in there and squish the mixture together for several minutes, to ensure it is very well combined.

Divide the mixture into six equal portions, then roll each into a log about 30 cm (12 inches) long and 3 cm (1¼ inches) in diameter. Place on a tray lined with baking paper, then cover and set aside in the refrigerator while you roll out your pastry.

To roll out the pastry, and assemble and bake the rolls, follow the instructions for the Good 'n' savoury sausage rolls recipe on page 166.

Serve hot, with tomato sauce if desired.

Apple pies with fresh cream

Fancy that!

You can add raisins or sultanas (golden raisins) to the apple filling, and some toasted chopped nuts too, if desired. You can also substitute pears for the apple.

Sure there was 'I spy with my little eye' to keep us entertained on long family car trips, but I was always more interested in where we'd stop to eat. I have a strong memory of one pie shop that dad would make a B-line to on a certain route. Not the name of it, where it was or even the general direction — just the crunch of sugar on top of the tender pie pastry, the not-too-sweet real apple filling, the pure fresh cream, which was rare in those days — and the look of satisfaction on my dad's face. He was likely looking at my own at the time.

Makes 6 individual pies

8 granny smith apples

80 g (2¾ oz) unsalted butter

1 teaspoon ground cinnamon

a good couple of pinches of freshly grated nutmeg, or ground cloves, ginger or cardamom (optional)

110 g (3¾ oz/½ cup) caster (superfine) sugar

100 g (3½ oz/½ cup) brown sugar

2 tablespoons cornflour (cornstarch)

80 ml (2½ fl oz/⅓ cup) good-quality unfiltered apple juice

1 quantity of Sweet shortcrust pastry (page 224), or 3 sheets frozen ready-rolled sweet shortcrust pastry, thawed

milk, for brushing

raw sugar, for sprinkling

whipped cream or vanilla ice cream, to serve (optional)

Peel, core and quarter the apples, then cut the quarters into slices 8 mm (⅜ inch) thick. Melt the butter in a large frying pan over medium heat. Add the apple slices, spices, caster sugar and brown sugar. Cook, stirring occasionally, for 10–12 minutes, or until the apple has wilted slightly.

Mix together the cornflour and apple juice until smooth, then pour into the apple mixture, stirring well to combine. Cook, stirring gently, for a further 40–60 seconds, or until the apple is tender and the sauce has thickened. Transfer the filling to a bowl, cool slightly, then cover and refrigerate until cold.

Meanwhile, roll out two-thirds of the pastry to a 2–3 mm (¹⁄₁₆–⅛ inch) thickness, then cut out six 15 cm (6 inch) rounds. Take six lightly greased individual non-stick pie tins, measuring about 12 cm (4½ inches) across the top, 8 cm (3¼ inches) across the base and 3.5 cm (1½ inches) deep at the sides. Line the tins with the pastry, pressing the pastry lightly into the edges; allow the pastry to come up over the edges of the pie tin, then press it down onto the rims. Use a sharp knife to trim around the outside edge, so the pastry is neat against the rim of the tin. Chill until your filling is cold.

When ready to bake the pies, place two baking trays in the oven and preheat it to 200°C (400°F).

Divide the chilled filling among the pastry shells. Roll the remaining pastry out to 5 mm (¼ inch) thick, then cut out six 13.5 cm (5½ inch) rounds, using a round of baking paper as your guide. Top the pies with the lids, then pinch or crimp the edges of the top and bottom pastry layers to seal. Brush the top of the pies with milk, sprinkle with raw sugar and poke a small air vent in the top of each one.

Place on the hot baking trays, close the oven door and immediately turn the temperature down to 180°C (350°F). Bake for 40–45 minutes, or until the pastry is golden and the filling is hot.

Serve warm with whipped cream or vanilla ice cream on the side... or wait until the pies are at room temperature and pipe a big rosette of cream on top before serving — that's how I remember them being served in the shop!

The pies are best eaten on day of baking. If making ahead of time, you can store them in a single layer in an airtight container in the fridge for up to 3 days, then gently reheat in the oven until the pastry crisps up and the filling is heated through.

Custard tarts

If it wasn't an apple pie for dad, it was a custard tart, and if the number of vanilla-scented crushed foil pie tins and paper bags in his car was any indication, they were wolfed down with a certain regularity. The trick here is to almost undercook the custard; I'm talking shimmy-smooth and glistening with a good hit of fresh, aromatic nutmeg. For a coconut cream version, use coconut milk and cream instead of dairy milk and cream.

Makes 6 individual tarts

1 quantity of Sweet shortcrust pastry (page 224), or 3 sheets frozen ready-rolled sweet shortcrust pastry, thawed

1 vanilla bean

500 ml (17 fl oz/2 cups) thin (pouring) cream

185 ml (6 fl oz/¾ cup) full-cream milk

8 egg yolks

4 whole eggs

165 g (5¾ oz/¾ cup) caster (superfine) sugar

50 g (1¾ oz/¼ cup) brown sugar

freshly grated nutmeg, for sprinkling

Lightly grease six individual pie tins, measuring about 12 cm (4½ inches) across the top, 8 cm (3¼ inches) across the base and 3.5 cm (1½ inches) deep.

Roll the pastry out to a 3 mm (⅛ inch) thickness. With the tip of a sharp knife, cut out six 15 cm (6 inch) diameter rounds. (If you are not comfortable doing this freehand, you may like to trace this size round onto some baking paper, cut it out with scissors then use it as a template.)

Carefully press each pastry round into the bottom of one of the pie tins. Trim off any overhanging pastry using a sharp knife, then pinch around the edges if you like. Refrigerate for 30 minutes.

Preheat the oven to 190°C (375°F). Place the pie tins on two baking trays. Line each pastry shell with a square of baking paper, then cover the base with pie weights, baking beads or uncooked rice. Blind-bake for 8 minutes, then remove the paper and weights and bake for a further 5–6 minutes, or until the pastry is pale golden and dry all over.

Remove the baking trays from the oven. Turn the oven temperature down to 160°C (315°F).

Using a small sharp knife, split the vanilla bean down its length, scrape out the seeds, then place both the pod and seeds in a saucepan. Add the cream and milk and bring to the boil over medium–high heat. Remove from the heat and allow to infuse for 15 minutes.

Meanwhile, in a bowl, whisk the egg yolks, eggs and sugar together until smooth and pale. Gradually whisk the milk mixture into the egg mixture until smooth, then strain into a jug. Carefully divide the custard mixture among the pastry shells. Sprinkle with freshly grated nutmeg.

Bake for 30–35 minutes, or until the custard is dry on top, but still a little wobbly when you gently tap the baking tray. Remove from the oven and allow the tarts to cool in the pie tins. Serve warm or chilled.

If you're not serving the tarts straight away, wait until they've cooled, then store them in a single layer in an airtight container. They will keep in the fridge for up to 4 days.

For variety, divide the following ingredients among the blind-baked pastry shells before pouring the custard in.

Afternoon tea

A little lemon zest, and 90 g (3¼ oz) raisins, sultanas (golden raisins), dates or prunes that have been soaked overnight in strong black tea.

Dark & dreamy

30 g (1 oz) finely chopped dark chocolate, and 90 g (3¼ oz) raisins, sultanas (golden raisins), dates or prunes that have been soaked overnight in dark rum or dark, rich sherry.

Red & white with bite

30 g (1 oz) chopped white chocolate, and 90 g (3¼ oz) dried tart cherries or cranberries soaked overnight in cherry liqueur or brandy.

NOTE *You can also make one large custard tart, rather than individual ones, using a loose-based 26 cm (10½ inch) diameter, 5 cm (2 inch) deep pie dish. Line the dish with the pastry and blind-bake for about 10 minutes, then remove the baking paper and weights and bake for a further 8–10 minutes, or until the pastry is pale golden and dry all over. Fill with the custard and cook for about 50 minutes. Leave to cool in the pie dish.*

Vanilla slice

Makes 10 rich vanilla slices

⅓ quantity of Puff pastry (page 225),
rolled to a 2 mm (1⁄16 inch) thickness
and cut into two 23 cm (9 inch)
squares, or 2 sheets ready-rolled
frozen puff pastry, thawed

mild-flavoured cooking oil spray

1½ quantities of freshly made Crème
pâtissière (page 61), still warm

Passionfruit icing

185 g (6½ oz/1½ cups) icing
(confectioners') sugar

1 tablespoon unsalted butter, melted
and cooled

2 tablespoons passionfruit pulp

2 teaspoons boiling water

Preheat the oven to 220°C (425°F). Place each pastry sheet on a large, lightly greased baking tray, prick all over with a fork, then sit another clean baking tray on top to weigh the pastry down slightly, making it rise evenly. Bake for 20–25 minutes, or until deep golden all over. Allow to cool completely on the baking trays, placed on wire racks, then trim the edges so that each pastry sheet will fit into a 22–23 cm (8½–9 inch) square cake tin.

Lightly spray the base of your cake tin with cooking oil spray. Line the base with a sheet of baking paper long enough to come up the sides and well overhang them — this is important, as it will help you lift the vanilla slice out of the tin once the custard layer has set.

Gently fit a pastry sheet into the base of the tin, then dollop the warm crème pâtissière over the top, smoothing the surface so it is level. Top with the second sheet of pastry, with the flattest side facing up. Press down slightly to help it adhere to the custard, then refrigerate for several hours, or until the custard is completely cold and more firm.

When you are ready to ice the top, make the passionfruit icing by mixing all the ingredients together until smooth. The icing should have a slightly flowing, spreadable consistency. Pour the icing over the top of the pastry and use a crank-handled or offset spatula to spread it evenly to the edges. Return to the fridge and allow to set for about 1 hour or so.

When ready to serve, lift the vanilla slice out of the tin and onto your work surface, using your baking-paper handles. Use a long, sharp, serrated knife to cut the slice into 10 even, rectangular pieces.

Serve with a dessert fork, as the custard is a little softer than one that has been set firm with gelatine… and so it may squeeze out the sides and down your front when you bite down!

If you're not serving the slice straight away, store it in a single layer in an airtight container. It will keep in the fridge for up to 4 days.

The matchstick

Follow the recipe above as a guide, but use three layers of pastry instead of two. Spread the bottom layer with jam of your choice. Top with a 2 cm (¾ inch) thick layer of whipped cream or warm Crème pâtissière (page 61); repeat with another layer of pastry, jam and cream or Crème pâtissière. Top with the third pastry sheet and spread with Vanilla icing (from the Neenish tarts recipe on page 177). Quickly pipe two parallel lines of Chocolate icing (Neenish tarts, page 177) down the length of the slice. Working quickly, and starting at one end, use a skewer to cross horizontally over the icings one way, then back in the opposite way, at even intervals all the way down — probably best around 2 cm (¾ inch) apart.

Also known as custard slice, Napoleon slice, and the far less appetising 'snot block' (which I hate!), there have been several incarnations of the vanilla slice over the decades. The average vanilla slice is a dessert constructed of a rather firm-set, almost fluorescent gelatinous 'custard' sandwiched between puff pastry layers — a rather loose rendition of the French *gateau de mille-feuille* ('thousand layer cake'). In the 1980s, a growing number of fancy patisseries inadvertently started influencing traditional pie shops and bakeries to include real crème pâtissière in their vanilla slices. Some were aerated with whipped cream, while others evolved into double-deckered whipped cream and crème pâtissière constructions. Ooh la lah.

Even though I find most versions of these tarts way too sweet, they are such a fond childhood memory that I'll buy one for old time's sake every now and again. They remind me of my grandmother and the store I used to visit on the way to her house after high school — I'd always pick up something nice for afternoon tea when Nana's once-fabulous baking skills were stolen by dementia; the mouldy slice with random dubious ingredients simply wasn't worth the risk... Tradition or perhaps fiscally challenging times or even storage issues dictated that Neenish, Nenish or Nienich tarts, possibly named after a baker of the same name, are filled with mock cream, but I've also given a fresh cream version here.

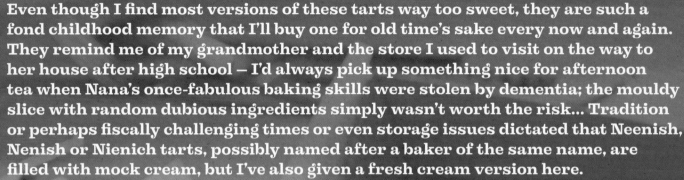

Pineapple tarts

You'll often find these nestled next to the Neenish tarts, like the kissing cousins they are. Same tart, different jam and icing — that's it. Simply use pineapple jam instead of berry jam on the pastry base, and a single passionfruit icing to top them — see Vanilla slice, page 174, for the recipe.

Pineapple jam is more easily found in speciality food stores than the supermarket, but well worth seeking out. It's also great with home-made Peanut butter (page 221) on toast.

Makes 16 tartlets

1 quantity of Sweet shortcrust pastry (page 224), or 4 sheets ready-rolled sweet shortcrust pastry

1 tablespoon strawberry, raspberry, blackberry or cherry jam

Fresh cream filling

200 ml (7 fl oz) thin (pouring) cream

40 g (1½ oz/⅓ cup) icing (confectioners') sugar

1 teaspoon pure vanilla extract

Mock cream filling alternative

2 tablespoons full-cream milk

110 g (3¾ oz/½ cup) caster (superfine) sugar

½ teaspoon gelatine powder, dissolved in 1 teaspoon boiling water

150 g (5½ oz) unsalted butter, chopped

1 teaspoon pure vanilla extract

Vanilla icing

105 g (3¾ oz/heaped ¾ cup) icing (confectioners') sugar, sifted

¼ teaspoon pure vanilla extract

3–4 teaspoons boiling water

Chocolate icing

90 g (3¼ oz/¾ cup) icing (confectioners') sugar, sifted

2 teaspoons good-quality unsweetened cocoa powder

1 tablespoon boiling water

Lightly grease a 16-hole patty pan or small muffin tin; you want the holes to be about 7 cm (2¾ inches) across the top, 4 cm (1½ inches) across the base, and about 2.5 cm (1 inch) deep, with outward sloping sides.

Roll the pastry out to a 2 mm (1/16 inch) thickness. Cut out 9 cm (3½ inch) rounds with a cookie cutter or pastry cutter. Line each tin hole with the pastry rounds, pressing gently into and around the edges, and gently pushing the pastry up about 5 mm (¼ inch) above the rim of the tin, all the way around. Prick the bases with a fork and refrigerate for 30 minutes.

Meanwhile, preheat the oven to 180°C (350°F).

Bake the pastry cases for 10–12 minutes, or until lightly golden. Leave to cool in the baking tin on a wire rack until completely cold.

If using the fresh cream filling, whisk the cream, icing sugar and vanilla together until firmly whipped. Refrigerate for 2 hours, to ensure the mixture is really cold when you fill the tartlets.

If using the mock cream filling, put the milk, sugar and 2 tablespoons water in a small saucepan and stir over medium–high heat until the sugar has dissolved. Do not allow to boil. Remove from the heat and immediately whisk in the dissolved gelatine and cool until lukewarm. While the mixture is cooling, use an electric mixer to beat the butter and vanilla in a bowl until pale and airy. When the milk syrup is at the right temperature, turn the beaters back on to high and beat continuously as you gradually add in the syrup. Keep beating until light and fluffy; this will take about 8 minutes.

Remove the cold tart shells from the baking tin. Place ¼ teaspoon of jam in the bottom of each, then top with the fresh cream or mock cream filling, making sure it comes right level with the edge of the pastry. Smooth it over so the filling is flat. Refrigerate for 45 minutes, to ensure the tops are firm enough to ice.

Put all the vanilla icing ingredients in a bowl and whisk until smooth and cooled to room temperature; the icing should be fairly thick. Remove your tarts from the fridge and use a small palette knife to spread the vanilla icing over the top of two-thirds of the tart, in one smooth sweep. Refrigerate until set.

Now put all the chocolate icing ingredients in a bowl and whisk until smooth and cooled to room temperature. Remove your tarts from the fridge.

Using a small clean palette knife, and working from the uncovered side, spread the chocolate icing over half the tart, in one smooth sweep; the chocolate icing will overlap the vanilla icing in the middle of the tart. Try to keep it as neat as possible, so there is a distinct line between the dark and white icings.

Refrigerate until set. Then, after all your hard work, you are ready to serve and eat them!

If you're not serving the tarts straight away, wait until they've set, then store them in a single layer in an airtight container. They will keep in the fridge for up to 5 days.

Chapter 5

FISH 'N' CHIP SHOP

BLUE SKIES, THE salty scent of the sea, paper wrapping rustlings, a spritz of lemon, crunching into golden batter, seagulls squawking overhead and the promise of ice cream for dessert: childhood summer holiday memories on steroids. While there seemed to be plenty of great places for fish and chips when I was a kid — or perhaps I had lower standards back then — there is certainly a dearth of really decent fry-joints these days. All too often we are let down by bland fish in soggy batter cooked in stale, smelly oil, served with cheap, overly sweet condiments. A good tartare or cocktail sauce can make or break your fish and chip dinner. Reality.

Quality fish cooked just right is magic; over or undercooked and it is more than a little bit wrong. Many of the following recipes are so simple they'll have you scratching your head as to why you've been bothering with the grease-mongers down the road! You'll find all your old favourites here… and hopefully a few new ones too.

Getting fancy with your fish

Add sparing amounts of the following herbs or spices to your batter, being careful not to mask the natural flavour of your fish. Accompany with the suggested sauces.

• Cayenne pepper + smoked sweet paprika. Serve with Aïoli (page 231).

• Curry powder; serve with minted yoghurt and lemon.

• Fresh oregano + ground cumin. Serve with a lime-spiked Mayonnaise (page 231).

• Ground celery seeds + aniseed. Serve with Mayonnaise (page 231) seasoned with cider vinegar and dill.

• Nori flakes; serve with Mayonnaise (page 231) seasoned with soy sauce and mirin.

Golden battered fish

For me, the most crisp and delicious batters for fish are those containing some form of carbonation, and the easiest way to add this is in the form of an unsweetened fizzy liquid, such as soda water or beer. Clearly these two fizzy options have very different flavours — and while your fish won't taste like ale, beer batter does provide a deeper, more savoury flavour than soda water. You could also use champagne, but why would you waste it?

Serves 4–6 as a main, with chips and salad

800 g (1 lb 12 oz) skinless, boneless fish fillets of your choice — I prefer snapper, flathead or ling as I like a mild-flavoured white fish, but choose your favourite seasonal variety

mild-flavoured oil, such as sunflower or safflower, for deep-frying

fine sea salt, for sprinkling

lemon wedges or malt vinegar, to serve

Tartare sauce (page 230), to serve (optional)

Batter

225 g (8 oz/1½ cups) plain (all-purpose) flour

1 teaspoon fine sea salt

a good pinch of ground spices or chopped fresh herbs (optional; see 'Getting fancy with your fish', left)

330 ml (11¼ fl oz/1⅓ cups) chilled soda water (club soda) or beer

If you choose a fish with a wide fillet, you may like to cut the fillets in half lengthways to form thin fillets. Ideally, each piece of fish should be about 4 cm (1½ inches) wide and about 15 cm (6 inches) long — but this is only a guide, as each fish will vary.

When you're ready to cook, one-third fill a deep-fryer or large heavy-based saucepan with oil and heat to 180°C (350°F), or until a cube of bread dropped into the oil turns golden brown in 15 seconds.

To make the batter, put the flour and salt in a bowl with the spices or herbs, if using, then gradually mix in the soda water or beer until the batter is smooth and liquid, but thick enough to coat the fish fillets. You may not need to add the full quantity of liquid, as flour can contain more or less liquid depending on the weather. You may also need to

add a little extra liquid towards the end when the batter is running low, as it will thicken on standing.

Dip the fish fillets into the batter, allowing any excess batter to drip back into the bowl. Cook the fish in batches for 5 minutes, or until the batter is crisp and golden, and the fish is just cooked through. The timing may vary slightly depending on the thickness of your fish — a thicker fillet may take 1–2 minutes longer.

Drain on paper towel and sprinkle lightly with fine sea salt. Keep warm in a low oven while you finish cooking the remaining fish.

Serve with lemon wedges or malt vinegar for sprinkling over, and your choice of accompaniments, such as tartare sauce for dipping into, and hot chips (pages 196 and 199) and/or salad.

Crumbed fish

You can choose to deep-fry or shallow-fry crumbed fish in a large frying pan, but I find deep-frying results in a more consistent colour and texture, plus there is less risk of the fish breaking up when flipping it over in your frying pan.

Serves 4–6 as a main with sides

150 g (5½ oz/1 cup) plain
(all-purpose) flour

ground white pepper, for seasoning

2 large eggs

210 g (7½ oz/3½ cups) breadcrumbs,
made from day-old bread

800 g (1 lb 12 oz) skinless, boneless
fish fillets — the choice of fish
is yours

mild-flavoured oil, for frying

fine sea salt, for seasoning

lemon wedges, to serve

Tartare sauce (page 230), to serve
(optional)

Spread the flour on a plate, season with sea salt and ground white pepper and mix together well. In a wide flat bowl, lightly beat the eggs. Spread the breadcrumbs on a plate.

Working with one fish fillet at a time, lightly coat in the seasoned flour. Shake off any excess, then dip into the beaten egg, ensuring the fish is coated well, and allowing any excess egg to drop back into the bowl. Place the fish on the plate of crumbs and gently press down to help adhere; turn the fish over and press the crumbs onto the other side.

Line a tray with baking paper and sprinkle with a thick layer of the remaining breadcrumbs. Place the crumbed fish on the tray, cover lightly with plastic wrap and refrigerate for about 1 hour, to help the crumbs adhere to the fish.

When ready to cook

If deep-frying, one-third fill a deep-fryer or large heavy-based saucepan with oil and heat to 180°C (350°F), or until a cube of bread dropped into the oil turns golden brown in 15 seconds. Cook the fish in batches for 4–5 minutes, or until the crumbs are golden and the fish is just cooked through. Drain on paper towel, sprinkle with fine sea salt and serve or keep warm in a low oven while you finish cooking the rest of the fish.

If shallow-frying, heat about 1 cm (½ inch) of oil in a large frying pan, over medium–high heat. Cook the fish in batches for 2–3 minutes on each side, or until the crumbs are lightly golden and the fish is cooked through; it should be opaque and flake easily with a fork. Drain on paper towel, season with a little fine sea salt and serve or keep warm in a low oven while you cook the rest of the fish.

Serve warm, with lemon wedges and tartare sauce, if using. Ideal sides are Double-crunch hot chips (page 199) or Shoestring fries (page 196), or boiled baby potatoes, and/or a green salad or steamed green beans.

You don't have to stick to breadcrumbs in your crumb coating — try substituting with polenta, or adding finely chopped nuts, shredded coconut, or small seeds such as sesame or poppy seeds. If you are gluten/wheat intolerant, you can even use these ingredients instead of breadcrumbs. You can also add a little grated hard cheese (such as parmesan or pecorino) to your crumbs, and/or a hint of ground spices or finely chopped fresh herbs for flavour.

You don't want to mask the flavour of the fish, so go sparingly on white-fleshed fish — just enough to add a hint of additional flavour. For salmon, tuna and oilier fish you can be a little more generous with your seasoning. For even more flavour, you can also add aromatics such as garlic or ginger to the egg wash — again, best for deeper-flavoured fish.

Try adding the following to your crumb coating.

very finely chopped parsley + lemon zest + capers

•

finely chopped almonds + paprika + ground cumin

•

finely grated parmesan + shredded basil

•

finely chopped macadamia nuts + chilli powder + lime zest

•

finely chopped almonds + sage + nutmeg

•

very finely chopped hazelnuts + thyme + lemon zest

•

shredded coconut + ground coriander + finely chopped coriander (cilantro) leaf

•

finely chopped mint + sesame seeds + ground allspice + ground cumin

Calamari rings

I'm a sucker for a good calamari ring — a light crunch in the coating, and tender flesh with just a hint of resistance on the inside. Timed just right and seasoned to perfection, calamari rings are almost like the 'chip' of the fish world, and an essential part of any fisherman's basket worth its salt — but how often they disappoint! Not these ones, though. Give them a whirl.

Serves 4-6 as a snack or starter

2 cleaned calamari (squid) hoods, 300 g (10½ oz) each — never fear if they are frozen, as this helps tenderise the flesh

2 eggs, lightly beaten

300 g (10½ oz/5 cups) breadcrumbs, made from day-old bread, or 300 g (10½ oz/3 cups) almond meal (or use half/half)

mild-flavoured oil, for deep-frying

fine sea salt, for sprinkling

lemon wedges, to serve

Tartare sauce (page 230), Cocktail sauce (page 230) or Aïoli (page 231), for dipping (optional)

Marinade

500 ml (17 fl oz/2 cups) buttermilk

5 garlic cloves, finely sliced

3 large thyme sprigs, finely chopped

Spiced flour

150 g (5½ oz/1 cup) plain (all-purpose) flour

1 tablespoon sweet paprika

½ teaspoon cayenne pepper

a good pinch of ground cloves

With your thumb, rub the outside of the wide rim of each calamari hood opening, until you have worn away some of the very fine membrane that covers the hood; this is easier to do if your calamari is semi-frozen. From here you can peel off the skin and discard. You don't have to do this step, but if you do, it will avoid those weird stringy rubber band-like bits you sometimes find with calamari rings.

Using a sharp knife, cut the hoods into rings about 6 mm (¼ inch) wide. Combine the marinade ingredients in a non-metallic bowl (there's a natural acid in the buttermilk, which will tenderise the calamari, but it can also react with metal and taint the colour and flavour of the calamari). Add the calamari rings, coating all over. Cover and refrigerate for at least 6 hours, or overnight.

When ready to coat the calamari, drain and discard the marinade. Lightly beat the eggs in a wide shallow bowl. Spread the breadcrumbs or almond meal on a plate, and combine the spiced flour ingredients in a bowl.

Toss the calamari rings through the spiced flour, coating them all over, then shake off any excess. Dip the calamari, just a few rings at a time, in the egg, allowing any excess egg to drip back into the bowl, then press down into the breadcrumbs on both sides. Place on a lined tray and repeat with all the rings. Sprinkle any leftover breadcrumbs over the top. Cover and refrigerate for 1–2 hours, to help the coating adhere to the calamari.

When you're ready to cook, one-third fill a deep-fryer or large heavy-based saucepan with oil and heat to 190°C (375°F), or until a cube of bread dropped into the oil turns golden brown in 10 seconds.

Cook the calamari in batches for 1 minute per batch, or until golden and cooked through. Drain on paper towel and sprinkle with a little sea salt. Best served immediately, however you can keep the rings warm in a low oven while you finish frying the rest, if you like.

Serve with lemon wedges, and your choice of dipping sauce, if using.

If you find yourself craving Chinese takeaway, spice things up a little with a batch of **salt & pepper calamari**. Simply omit the thyme from the buttermilk marinade and increase the garlic to 7 cloves. Lightly dredge the drained calamari in plain (all-purpose) flour. Whisk together 250 ml (9 fl oz/ 1 cup) cold sparkling water, 1 teaspoon baking powder, 100 g (3½ oz/⅔ cup) plain flour, 3 teaspoons Chinese five-spice powder, 1½ teaspoons ground sichuan pepper, 1½ teaspoons ground white pepper and 1 teaspoon ground black pepper to make a batter. Dip the rings in the batter and allow the excess to drip off. Fry in small batches at 190°C (375°F) for 1 minute. Drain, then season with sea salt and a little extra sichuan pepper if desired. If you like, serve with Mayonnaise (page 231) mixed with hoisin sauce and a little black rice vinegar.

You can also make **salt & pepper prawns** (shrimp) the same way.

Fish cakes

Fish can be rudely expensive these days, but it's important to include it in our diets. This delicious recipe using quality tinned tuna or salmon provides an economical way to 'get it in you'. Buy a reputable, ethical brand if possible, then enjoy these fish cakes with salad and chippies, or in a fish burger. For four decades I detested fish cakes; in fact I long considered anything containing tinned fish to be cat food. Now I'm a born-again fish cake fanatic.

Makes 8 fish cakes; serves 4 as a main with sides

- 500 g (1 lb 2 oz) floury (roasting) or all-purpose potatoes, such as russet or desiree, washed but not peeled
- 1 small brown onion
- 185 g (6½ oz) tin tuna or salmon
- 1 celery stalk, very finely diced
- 2 teaspoons very finely chopped dill
- 1 tablespoon very finely chopped flat-leaf (Italian) parsley
- 2 teaspoons very finely chopped capers
- ¼ teaspoon very finely chopped lemon zest
- 1 egg, lightly beaten
- plain (all-purpose) flour, seasoned with salt and pepper, for dusting
- mild-flavoured oil, for shallow-frying
- sea salt flakes, for sprinkling
- lemon wedges, to serve
- Tartare sauce (page 230) or Aïoli (page 231), to serve (optional)

Put the potatoes in a saucepan and cover well with cold water. Bring to the boil and cook until very tender; the actual cooking time will depend on the size of your potatoes. Drain in a colander until cool enough to handle, then peel and mash in a large bowl.

Finely grate the onion and squeeze out any excess juice. Add to the potatoes. Drain and flake the fish and add to the bowl with the celery, herbs, capers, lemon and egg. Combine thoroughly. Season to taste with sea salt and freshly cracked black pepper, then cover and chill the mixture for 2 hours.

Taking about 90 g (3¼ oz/⅓ cup) of the mixture at a time, shape into round cakes about 7 cm (2¾ inches) in diameter, and 2 cm (¾ inch) thick. Coat well in the seasoned plain flour.

Heat 1.5 cm (⅝ inch) of oil in a large frying pan over medium–high heat. When the oil is nice and hot, cook the fish cakes for 2 minutes on each side, or until golden and heated through; depending on the size of your pan, you may need to cook them in two batches. Also note that the oil needs to be hot enough to form a crust, or the fish cakes will fall apart.

Drain on paper towel, sprinkle with sea salt flakes and serve hot, with lemon wedges and sauce of your choice.

You can make a meal of them by serving with your choice of hot chips (pages 196, 199) and/or a green salad.

Fish cake magic!

Curry-in-a-hurry fish cakes

Add 1½ teaspoons curry powder to the fish cake mixture; change the dill to coriander (cilantro) or mint, and omit the capers. Serve with yoghurt or Mayonnaise (page 231) mixed with a little chutney, and some extra coriander or mint.

Doin' it Italian-style fish cakes

Don't over-season your fish mixture, as these additions are quite salty! Add some chopped black olives to the fish cake mixture and swap the dill for basil. Serve with Aïoli (page 231) mixed with lemon, a little mashed anchovy, some finely grated parmesan cheese and more chopped basil.

French kiss fish cakes

Add a little finely chopped bacon to the fish mixture, replace the dill with French tarragon, and the capers with finely chopped cornichons. Serve with Aïoli (page 231).

Tripitaka's flippin' trippin' fish cakes

Add some nori flakes, finely chopped spring onion (scallion) and finely grated fresh ginger to the fish mixture; omit the dill and capers. Serve with Japanese (Kewpie) mayonnaise mixed with a pinch of dashi powder and toasted sesame seeds, a dash of soy sauce, a squeeze of lemon juice and some more finely chopped spring onion.

AHOY! FISHERMAN'S BASKET AHEAD

Instead of a barbecue next time you have a group of friends together for a casual summer al fresco dinner, why not make up a good old-fashioned fisherman's basket for each person? Borrow a couple of deep-fryers from neighbours. Line individual serving baskets with newspaper, then a smaller square of baking paper. Cook and season all your seafood, larger pieces first, and keep warm in a low oven while you cook the rest.

In each basket, arrange some Calamari rings (page 186), a piece of Golden battered fish (page 183), some Butterflied prawn cutlets (page 194), a couple of battered scallops (briefly deep-fried in the basic beer batter on page 183), perhaps some Seafood sticks (page 202), some Double-crunch hot chips (page 199) or a Potato scallop (page 206), and some lemon wedges. Put some small bowls of Tartare sauce (page 230), Cocktail sauce (page 230) or Aïoli (page 231) on a tray, with a bottle of malt vinegar for the table. And offer a large green salad.

Or, if you don't mind heading back to the kitchen a few times during dinner, serve the fish and chips first, then cook up some prawns (shrimp) and calamari in separate batches and pass them around on a platter for guests to add to their baskets as they are cooked. They'll be hotter and more crisp this way too!

This is such a fun way to celebrate summer and relive a few childhood memories. And I'm betting it'll be the best damn fisherman's basket you've had in years!

Flavoured butters

A nice little nub of flavoured butter goes down a treat on grilled fish (see next page). The stronger-flavoured the fish, the more robustly flavoured butter it can take, so bear this in mind when preparing your butter mix. Here's what to do.

For 4–6 servings, soften 50 g (1¾ oz) of your favourite butter, then mix through about 2 tablespoons of whatever finely chopped soft, flavourful herbs or aromatics take your fancy (see right for ideas). Season to taste, roll into a sausage shape or pat into a rectangle, then wrap in plastic wrap and refrigerate until just before serving. Remove from the fridge as you are about to cook your fish and slice thinly. Top the cooked fish just before serving.

- *garlic + parsley + lemon zest*

- *capers + dill + lemon zest*

- *grated onion + chilli + lime zest + chopped coriander (cilantro)*

- *black olives + feta cheese + chopped oregano + lemon zest*

- *smoked paprika + tomato paste (concentrated purée) + chopped garlic + chilli*

- *chopped fresh basil + garlic + lemon zest + chilli*

- *chopped coriander (cilantro) + spring onion (scallion) + Chinese five-spice + a touch of sesame oil*

Grilled fish

For most of my childhood, simply grilled fish was not so readily available from fish and chip joints. However, in the late 1980s, a few high-end fish shops opened up, catering to a more health-conscious audience, who could choose their cut of fish and how they liked it cooked. Grilling is not only the simplest way to serve fish, but is also the easiest way to cook it — although you do have to be careful not to overcook the fish, as it can dry out easily.

Serves 4–6 as a main with sides

800 g (1 lb 12 oz) fish fillets, skin on or off; leaving the skin on helps stop the fish falling apart when you turn it over, but does impart a stronger flavour

mild-flavoured oil or melted butter, for brushing

fine sea salt, for sprinkling

your choice of flavoured butter, to serve (optional; see previous page)

snipped chives or finely chopped soft fresh herbs such as chervil, tarragon or parsley, for sprinkling (optional)

lemon wedges, to serve

hot chips (pages 196 or 199) and/or salad, to serve

Preheat your grill (broiler) to high. Line a grill tray or baking tray with baking paper.

Place the fish fillets, skin side down if they have skin on, on the tray, spacing them slightly apart. Brush lightly with the oil or butter, sprinkle with fine sea salt and place under the grill.

Cook for 2–3 minutes, or until a little opaque, then carefully turn the fish over and cook for a further 2–4 minutes, or until the flesh is opaque and lightly golden, and flakes easily with a fork. The actual cooking time will depend on the thickness of your fillets, but as a general rule a thinner fish fillet like snapper or ling will only take 2–3 minutes per side, while a thicker fillet like salmon, tuna or swordfish make take around 4–6 minutes per side. If the fish has skin, you may also need to give it a little longer under the grill to crisp up than skinless fillets.

Transfer to serving plates, then top with flavoured butter or sprinkle with herbs if desired. Add a wedge of lemon to each plate. Serve with hot chips and/or salad.

HOT TIP *You can also grill (broil) one side of the skinless fish fillets, then flip them over, top the uncooked side with plain or seasoned breadcrumbs (see page 185), drizzle with melted butter and place under a medium–hot grill until the crumbs are golden and the fish is cooked through.*

Butterflied prawn cutlets

Not just for Chinese takeaways, you know. An essential component of any self-respecting Fisherman's basket (page 190), these cutlets are also great on their own, as a mighty fine finger food.

Makes 24

24 raw king prawns (shrimp)

75 g (2¾ oz/½ cup) plain (all-purpose) flour

2 eggs, lightly beaten

90 g (3¼ oz/1½ cups) breadcrumbs, made from two-day-old bread

vegetable or peanut oil, for deep-frying

fine sea salt, for sprinkling

lemon wedges, to serve

Tartare sauce (page 230) or Cocktail sauce (page 230), for dipping (optional)

Peel the prawns, leaving the tails attached. Take a small sharp knife and cut a line along the back of each prawn, where you can see the digestive tract — from the tail end to the head end. Make sure you don't cut right through the prawn — just three-quarters of the way. Remove the digestive tract and discard.

Use your fingers to open the prawns up from the incision and flatten them down. Now use a rolling pin or the back of a heavy knife to gently beat the prawns out a little more, so that they lay flat, but don't beat them to the point of ripping the flesh.

Prepare three bowls, one of well-seasoned flour, one with beaten eggs and one with breadcrumbs. Individually dip the prawns in the flour, shaking off any excess. Dip into the egg, allowing any excess egg to drip back into the bowl, then cover with the breadcrumbs, pressing down lightly to help them adhere. Place on a tray lined with baking paper.

Repeat with all the prawns, then cover with plastic wrap and chill for at least 1 hour.

When ready to cook, one-third fill a deep-fryer or large heavy-based saucepan with oil and heat to 170°C (325°F), or until a cube of bread dropped into the oil turns golden brown in 20 seconds. Cook the prawns in batches for 2 minutes, or until golden and just cooked through. Drain on paper towel and sprinkle with fine sea salt. Serve with lemon wedges, and a dipping sauce if desired.

PRAWN STARS *Instead of using breadcrumbs, you can also use ground or finely chopped mild-flavoured nuts such as almonds, desiccated or shredded coconut, cornmeal, sesame seeds, or even crushed dried vermicelli noodles if you feel an Asian banquet coming on.*

Shoestring fries

Long ago, all chips were chunky, and often more soggy than crisp after they'd been steaming in the paper wrapping they were carted home in – but occasionally you'd find a fish shop or milkbar that ensured lots of good crunchy crusts through the chips, with soft, fluffy insides. I still fight with my brother for the crunchiest chips or potatoes in the bowl – his kids don't even get a look in!

The Double-crunch hot chips (page 199) are my favourites, but when the fast-food giants took off, so did the desire for 'French fries', a skinny cousin to the fat fish 'n' chip shop brutes – so if you're size-ist, these are for you! They look far more elegant than chunky chips, and you can pretend they are better for you – but in reality, more surface area is being fried, so I'll let you work that one out.

These ones are best dipped in a hot chocolate or caramel fudge sundae... Oh yes I did! Salt, sugar, fat: that magic combination.

Serves 4–6 as a side or snack

3 large russet potatoes, or other roasting or chipping potatoes, about 750 g (1 lb 10 oz) in total

mild-flavoured oil, for deep-frying

fine sea salt, Roast chicken salt (page 37) or Lemon, rosemary & garlic salt (page 37), for sprinkling

Peel the potatoes. Using a sharp knife, or a julienne blade on a food processor, cut the chips into strips about 5 mm (¼ inch) square in diameter, and as long as the potato. Place the cut chips in a bowl of cold water while you finish cutting the rest.

When you're ready to cook, one-third fill a deep-fryer or large heavy-based saucepan with oil and heat to 190°C (375°F), or until a cube of bread dropped into the oil turns golden brown in 10 seconds.

Meanwhile, drain the chips. Cover your work surface with clean, dry tea towels, then spread the chips out in a single layer to dry. Blot the top of the chips dry with paper towel.

When they're as dry as possible, cook the chips in batches for 3–4 minutes, or until crisp and cooked through. Drain and sprinkle with your choice of salt, then serve immediately or keep warm in a low oven while you cook the rest... if you can resist nibbling them as you go.

> **NICE SPICE** *Omit the rosemary. During the second roasting phase, sprinkle with some spices of your choice and toss to combine well. Good options include smoked paprika, ground cumin, ground coriander, fennel seeds, caraway seeds, celery seeds, curry powder or a touch of Chinese five-spice, but do consider what you are serving the potatoes with if they are forming part of a meal; you don't want your flavours to clash.*

Smashed potatoes

I can't say these were readily available when I was lurking around the local milkbar in my youth, but I wanted to include them as they are a great chippy-like side that I reckon rival most chips. Try 'em and see. They're great with a burger, grilled fish or even with a roast.

Serves 6 as a side or snack

- 2 kg (4 lb 8 oz) small Dutch cream, desiree or baby potatoes; if you use larger potatoes, just cut them in half after they have boiled
- 8 whole garlic cloves, in their skins (optional)
- a handful of small rosemary sprigs (optional)
- 125 ml (4 fl oz/½ cup) olive oil
- sea salt flakes, for sprinkling

Preheat the oven to 200°C (400°F).

Leaving the skins on, cook the potatoes in a saucepan of boiling water for 7 minutes, or until just starting to become tender. Drain.

Put the potatoes in a large roasting tin, with the garlic cloves and rosemary, if using. Pour two-thirds of the olive oil over and toss to coat well. Sprinkle evenly with sea salt flakes and roast for 20 minutes, or until the potatoes are a little golden and starting to soften more.

Remove the tray from the oven. Carefully turn the potatoes in the oil, then using a wide metal spatula, or similar utensil, carefully press down to squash the potatoes to about half their original thickness. Drizzle the remaining olive oil over.

Continue roasting for about 1 hour, turning occasionally, until they are golden, crisp and cooked through, with soft, fluffy centres.

Drain on paper towel. Season to taste with extra salt, if needed, and serve.

I'm of the view that a good chip has a substantial yet fragile golden, crunchy exterior, and an almost insignificant amount of fluffy potato inside. It is the crunch factor that makes them so more-ish. Chips should retain a faint hint of oil, which seemingly disappears as soon as you've noticed its luscious moisture; not greasy or soggy, just elegantly lubricating the shatter. I want a chip in which the crunch holds up when you're halfway through the bowl. Obsessed? Perhaps.

This chip is loosely based on Heston Blumenthal's research. Yeah, I know everyone copies his triple-cooked chips recipe, but with good reason. The science of cooking and chilling and recooking at various temperatures changes the structure of the potato cells in a way that most of us without a science degree will never understand, so just trust me, this recipe is worth the effort.

DOUBLE-CRUNCH

hot chips

Serves 4

4 large floury (roasting or chipping) potatoes, such as russet, king edward or coliban; they should weigh about 1 kg (2 lb 4 oz) all up

2 tablespoons sea salt

peanut or vegetable oil, for deep-frying; you can also use half oil and half lard or duck fat

fine sea salt, Roast chicken salt (page 37) or Lemon, rosemary & garlic salt (page 37), for sprinkling

malt vinegar, to serve (optional)

Preheat the oven to 170°C (325°F).

Peel the potatoes, then rinse. Using a large sharp knife, cut into thick, square chips, about 1.5 cm (⅝ inch) wide, and as long as the length of each potato. You can trim off the rounded ends of the potatoes for a more uniform look.

Spread the chips out evenly in a large roasting tin. Stir the sea salt into 2 litres (70 fl oz/8 cups) boiling water until dissolved, then pour over the potatoes. Cover tightly with foil and bake for 1 hour and 10 minutes, or until very tender, but not breaking apart.

Using a slotted fish lifter or spatula, carefully transfer the chips-to-be in a single layer onto your work surface, or several baking trays that have been lined with clean, dry tea towels. Loosely drape some tea towels across the top to help the potatoes steam as you leave them to cool to room temperature. Refrigerate for 2 hours, or until completely cold.

One-third fill a deep-fryer or large heavy-based saucepan with oil and heat to 140°C (275°F), or until a cube of bread dropped into the oil turns golden brown in 45–50 seconds. Cook the chips in batches for 6–8 minutes, or until pale gold in colour.

Drain on paper towel, cool to room temperature, then refrigerate again for at least a couple of hours, or overnight — the chips must be completely cold. Allow your oil to cool in the pan, then cover if not using until the next day.

When ready to give the chips their final frying, heat the oil to 205°C (400°F), or until a cube of bread dropped into the oil turns golden brown in 5 seconds.

In batches, add the chips. The temperature will drop to about 180°C (350°F), so try to keep it consistently at this heat. Cook each batch for 4–5 minutes, or until deep gold and crunchy crisp. Drain on paper towel and sprinkle with your choice of salt. Serve with malt vinegar for traditionalists.

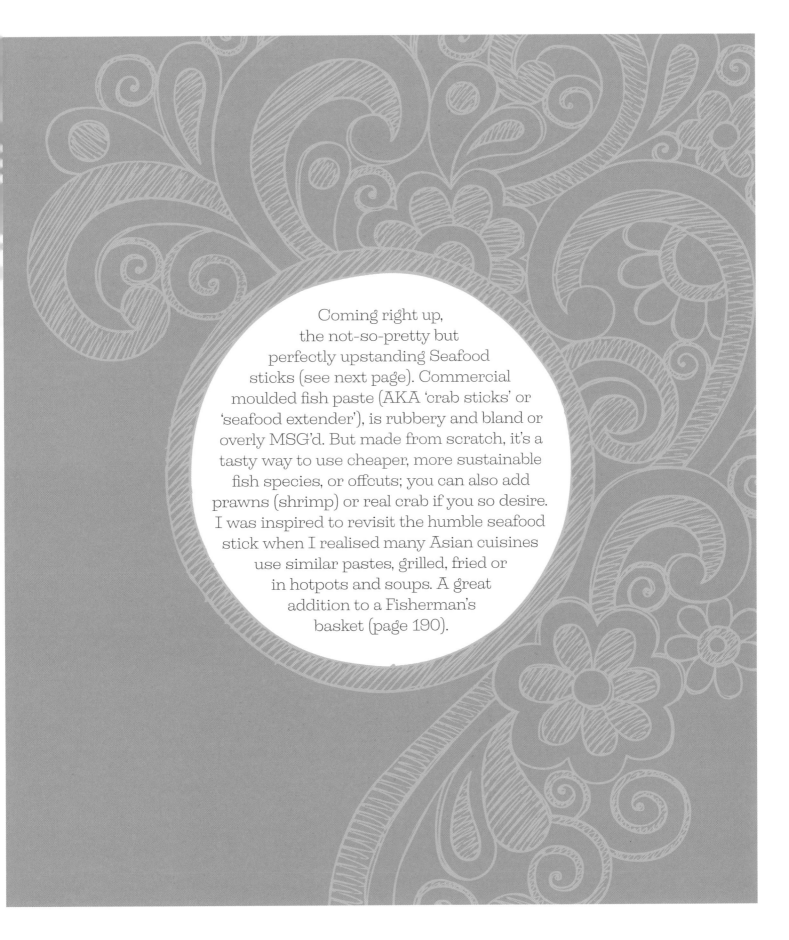

Coming right up, the not-so-pretty but perfectly upstanding Seafood sticks (see next page). Commercial moulded fish paste (AKA 'crab sticks' or 'seafood extender'), is rubbery and bland or overly MSG'd. But made from scratch, it's a tasty way to use cheaper, more sustainable fish species, or offcuts; you can also add prawns (shrimp) or real crab if you so desire. I was inspired to revisit the humble seafood stick when I realised many Asian cuisines use similar pastes, grilled, fried or in hotpots and soups. A great addition to a Fisherman's basket (page 190).

Seafood sticks

Makes 12 sticks, 40 g (1½ oz each)

mild-flavoured oil,
  for deep-frying

¾ teaspoon fine sea salt

a pinch of ground white
  pepper

a couple of good pinches of
  dashi powder (optional)

sea salt flakes, for
  sprinkling

lemon wedges, to serve
  (optional)

Tartare sauce (page 230),
  Cocktail sauce (page 230),
  Mayonnaise (page 231),
  Aïoli (page 231) or
  soy sauce, for dipping
  (optional)

For the seafood sticks

400 g (14 oz) boneless
  white fish fillets, or
  half fish and half prawn
  (shrimp) meat (see Note)

3 tablespoons potato flour

2½ teaspoons caster
  (superfine) sugar

3 spring onions (scallions),
  white part only, very
  finely chopped

1 garlic clove

scant ¼ teaspoon very
  finely grated lemon zest

1 large egg white

Before making the seafood sticks, chill the bowl and blade of your food processor.

Quickly chop your seafood into small pieces and place in your chilled food processor bowl. Process on high speed just until the mixture becomes a smooth paste. Add the remaining seafood stick ingredients and blend until just combined. Tip into a non-metallic bowl, then cover and refrigerate for 2 hours.

When ready to cook, one-third fill a deep-fryer or large heavy-based saucepan with oil and heat to 170°C (325°F), or until a cube of bread dropped into the oil turns golden brown in 20 seconds.

While the oil is heating, line a tray with baking paper and set aside in the fridge. Add the salt, pepper and dashi, if using, to the fish paste mixture and combine thoroughly. Using lightly oiled hands, shape 40 g (1½ oz) of the mixture (about the size of a golf ball) into a 'stick' about 1.5 cm (⅝ inch) in diameter and 12 cm (4½ inches) long. Place on the tray in the fridge, as you repeat with all the mixture to make 12 seafood sticks.

When the oil is ready, cook the seafood sticks in batches for 3 minutes, or until puffed, deep golden and cooked right through. Drain on paper towel and sprinkle with sea salt flakes. Serve straight away with lemon wedges, and a dipping sauce if desired.

If not serving straight away, you can let the seafood sticks cool slightly after deep-frying them, then refrigerate in an airtight container for up to 2 days. To serve, heat the seafood sticks in a frying pan, or under the grill (broiler) until hot all the way through.

NOTE *I prefer to use a mix of white-fleshed fish and prawns or crabmeat.*

Stylish sticks

Steam it up

Instead of deep-frying them, you can also steam the seafood sticks until cooked through. Serve them straight away, or chill the steamed sticks until you're ready to serve, then barbecue, pan-fry or deep-fry them in a basic beer batter (see Golden battered fish, page 183).

Happy herbs

Add a couple of teaspoons of finely chopped fresh dill, parsley or coriander (cilantro) to the seafood stick mixture.

YOU-BEAUT! *onion rings*

I have a weakness (okay, clearly one of many) and it is a perfectly crisp, melt-in-the-mouth onion ring. There are far too many limp, stodgy onion loops in the world, and if you've only eaten them in a fast-food joint, then erase that memory and begin again with these, please. Packed full of savoury onion flavour and a hint of natural sweetness, these rings are completely addictive. Don't dare say I didn't warn you.

Serves 4

2 large brown onions

500 ml (17 fl oz/2 cups) buttermilk

several decent sprigs of fresh thyme or rosemary

4 fresh bay leaves, crumpled

mild-flavoured oil, for deep-frying

150 g (5½ oz/1 cup) plain (all-purpose) flour

1 teaspoon baking powder

1 teaspoon sweet spicy paprika

a large pinch of cayenne pepper

1½ teaspoons lemon juice

fine sea salt, for sprinkling

Peel the onions and trim off the ends. Slice the onions into discs about 1–1.5 cm (½–⅝ inch) wide, then gently pull each disc apart into rings.

Place the buttermilk in a non-metallic bowl. Roll the herb sprigs between your hands to release the oils, then add to the bowl with the crumpled bay leaves. Add the onion rings and use your fingers to gently mix, ensuring all the rings are covered in the buttermilk. Cover and refrigerate for 3 hours.

When you're ready to cook, one-third fill a deep-fryer or large heavy-based saucepan with oil and heat to 180°C (350°F), or until a cube of bread dropped into the oil turns golden brown in 15 seconds.

In a bowl, combine the flour, baking powder, paprika and cayenne pepper; season well with sea salt and freshly ground black pepper. Gradually mix in the lemon juice and 125 ml (4 fl oz/½ cup) water; you should have a smooth, thickish batter.

Pluck the herbs from the onion mix, then drain off all but 4 tablespoons of the buttermilk from the bowl. Add the onion rings and half the remaining buttermilk to the batter and gently mix until the rings have a light, even coating. That little bit of buttermilk should thin the batter out slightly to a good coating consistency, but you can add a little more if needed.

Lift the rings out of the batter, allowing any excess to drip back into the bowl. Cook in small batches — you don't want to overcrowd your pan — stirring occasionally for 1½–2 minutes, or until the batter is golden and crisp, and the onion is cooked through.

Drain on paper towel and sprinkle with fine sea salt if desired. Either serve each batch as they are cooked, or keep them warm in a low oven while cooking the remaining rings. Serve hot.

Sweet potato wedges

In the early to mid 1980s, chips went all gourmet. It was suddenly no longer cool to order a bowl of plain chips to share with friends at the local cafe — we were munching on wide-angled wedges with sour cream and sweet chilli sauce until we turned into wide-angled teenagers. Takeaway joints had no option but to start offering wedges as well as chips, or turn a loss, and plain old fish-shop chips with vinegar would have to wait until 2014 to make a hip comeback. Of course you can use regular ol' potatoes for wedges, but I love the flavour of roast sweet potato.

These wedges are great with a burger or steak sandwich, or as a mighty snack on their own; see the ideas opposite.

Serves 4–6 as a hearty snack or side

2 x 600 g (1 lb 5 oz) orange sweet potatoes; pick ones that are evenly sized and shaped

80 ml (2½ fl oz/⅓ cup) olive oil or mild-flavoured vegetable oil

fine sea salt, for sprinkling

sour cream, to serve

Chilli sauce (page 228), or ready-made sweet chilli sauce mixed with a little honey, for drizzling

2 tablespoons snipped fresh chives

Preheat the oven to 200°C (400°F). Leaving the skins on, cut each sweet potato into three even lengths, then cut each length in half lengthways. Now cut each piece into three wedges about 3 cm (1¼ inches) wide at the wide part (which should be the skin side). You should end up with 36 wedges.

Place in a bowl with the oil and sprinkle liberally with sea salt. Toss to coat evenly, then place the wedges in a roasting tin, skin side down.

Roast for about 1 hour, until the wedges are crisp and golden, with darker patches from the natural sugars caramelising on the outside, and soft in the middle. If your oven bakes unevenly, you may need to turn the roasting tin around halfway through cooking, but otherwise you don't need to stir or turn the wedges themselves, which can break them up.

Drain on paper towel. Sprinkle with a little more salt if needed.

Serve each portion in a bowl, with a dollop of sour cream, a drizzle of sweet chilli sauce and a sprinkling of chives — or check out the 'Wedge fest!' on the opposite page for more decadent serving suggestions.

WEDGE FEST!

Muchos nachos wedges

Put the hot, cooked wedges in a large heatproof serving dish, sprinkle with a little ground cumin and salt, then scatter with grated cheddar cheese. Place under a hot grill (broiler) until the cheese is all gooey and lightly golden. Dollop with sour cream, chilli sauce, sliced jalapeño chillies, and avocado mashed with fresh lime juice. Serve sprinkled with chopped fresh coriander (cilantro).

Pepperoni pizza wedges

Put the hot, cooked wedges in a large heatproof serving dish. Scatter with grated mozzarella cheese, and also a little finely julienned pepperoni if you like. Place under a hot grill (broiler) until the cheese is all gooey and lightly golden. Dot with warmed Tomato sauce (page 226) and scatter with shredded fresh basil.

Surfin' safari sundowner wedges

Put the hot, cooked wedges in a large heatproof serving dish. Drizzle with warmed Satay sauce (page 229) and scatter with diced cucumber and chopped fresh mint. Add a squeeze of lime and serve.

Zorba wedges

Put the hot, cooked wedges in a large heatproof serving dish. Sprinkle with ground cinnamon and scatter with crumbled feta cheese. Place under a hot grill (broiler) until the cheese is lightly golden. Scatter with chopped black olives and chopped fresh dill or oregano. Squeeze a little lemon juice over the top and garnish with freshly cracked black pepper.

Potato scallops

As a New South Welshperson, I may be struck down for not calling these 'potato cakes' or 'potato fritters', as they do in other parts of Australia and indeed the globe. 'Whatevs', as the cool kids say. Good potato scallops are fluffy on the inside, with super-crunchy exteriors — I don't really mind what you call them, just pass 'em to me!

Serves 4

3 large floury (roasting) potatoes, such as russet or king edward; about 750 g (1 lb 10 oz) in total

mild-flavoured oil, for deep-frying

225 g (8 oz/1½ cups) plain (all-purpose) flour

1 teaspoon sea salt

1½ teaspoons baking powder

375 ml (13 fl oz/1½ cups) sparkling mineral water, soda water (club soda) or beer

fine sea salt, for sprinkling

Preheat the oven to 180°C (350°F). Peel the potatoes and cut into slices 1 cm (½ inch) thick. Place in a roasting tin and cover well with boiling water. Cover tightly with foil and cook for 15 minutes, or until just beginning to become tender. Meanwhile, line your work surface with clean tea towels.

Remove the roasting tin from the oven. Carefully remove the foil, then allow to cool for 30 minutes.

Use a slotted spatula to carefully transfer the potato slices to your prepared bench, spreading them out in a single layer, then leave until cool and fairly dry to the touch. Keep an eye on them because if left too long they will discolour.

One-third fill a deep-fryer or large heavy-based saucepan with oil and heat to 180°C (350°F), or until a cube of bread dropped into the oil turns golden brown in 15 seconds.

Combine the flour, salt and baking powder in a bowl and make a well in the centre. Gradually pour in the mineral water or beer as you gently whisk to combine, until you have a smooth and thickish batter.

Working in batches, dip the potato slices into the batter and deep-fry for 7–8 minutes, or until the batter is deep golden and very crisp.

Drain on paper towel and sprinkle with fine sea salt. Serve immediately, or keep warm in a low oven while you cook the remaining potato scallops.

Battered savs

Although rarely heard of these days, the 'battered sav' — a saveloy sausage, coated in a yeasted batter and deep-fried — used to feature on every fish and chip shop menu in town, a tradition passed down from our British cousins.

For me the memory of this munch-as-you-walk, fast-food-on-a-stick, also known as the dagwood dog or pluto pup, is closely linked to the Sydney Royal Easter Show. I haven't been for many years, but from a very early age right into my twenties I visited the show religiously, and every year I knew exactly what I'd be eating. It was the one day I would indulge in the battered sav ritual — sadly, the idea of eating one was always so much more pleasant than actually consuming the uniformly greasy and disappointing beast. But it was part of the experience, of course, and kept the whole 'fun of the fair' fantasy alive.

If they made battered savs like this at the show, I might even consider a comeback! The home-made saveloy sausages taste a little like a frankfurt, and while they are skinless and not dyed red (shock horror!), you can also use them in home-made hot dogs — just pan-fry or grill them on the barbecue before eating.

Batter matters

You can also use the basic beer batter from the Golden battered fish recipe on page 183, but it will be a thin crisp batter, whereas this more traditional yeasted batter is slightly chewy.

Makes 16 battered saveloys

Saveloy sausages

1.25 kg (2 lb 12 oz) well-marbled minced (ground) pork

2 tablespoons fine sea salt

1 tablespoon ground white pepper

½–1 teaspoon cayenne powder, depending how spicy you like it

2 tablespoons onion powder

1 tablespoon ground nutmeg

3 teaspoons smoked sweet paprika

2 teaspoons ground coriander

2 teaspoons ground cinnamon

1 tablespoon ground sage

100 g (3½ oz/⅔ cup) plain (all-purpose) flour

Yeast batter

2 teaspoons active dried yeast

1 teaspoon sugar

1 teaspoon fine sea salt

300 g (10½ oz/2 cups) plain (all-purpose) flour, sifted, plus extra for dusting

625 ml (21½ fl oz/2½ cups) lukewarm water

mild-flavoured oil, for deep-frying

Tomato sauce (page 226), to serve

Place all the saveloy sausage ingredients in a food processor. Add 100 ml (3½ fl oz) water and process until the mixture is as smooth as possible. Cover and chill overnight for the flavours to develop.

Divide the saveloy mixture into 16 portions, each weighing 70 g (2½ oz) and about the size of a golf ball. Shape each portion into a sausage shape about 13 cm (5 inches) long, and 2.5 cm (1 inch) in diameter.

Line a large bamboo steamer with a few layers of baking paper. Use a skewer to poke a few holes in the top baking paper sheet, then place the sausages on top, in a single layer; you'll probably need to cook them in two batches. Line the lid of the steamer with a clean, dry tea towel and, with the tea towel fairly taut, place the lid securely on the base. The tea towel will overhang the edges a little, so fold the ends back over the top of the lid, so there is no risk of the tea towel catching fire.

Bring a large saucepan of water to the boil. Set the steamer over the top and steam the sausages for 5 minutes, or until cooked through. Remove from the heat and leave to cool. Pack the sausages into an airtight container, with baking paper between each layer. Refrigerate again overnight for the flavours to further develop.

An hour or so before you plan to serve the battered savs, make the batter. Stir the yeast, sugar and sifted flour together. Put the water in a wide bowl and gradually mix in the flour mixture until the mixture is smooth, and the consistency of thin (pouring) cream. Cover with plastic wrap and a tea towel and set aside in a warm place for 1 hour, or until the batter has doubled in size.

When you're ready to cook, one-third fill a deep-fryer or large heavy-based saucepan with oil and heat to 180°C (350°F), or until a cube of bread dropped into the oil turns golden brown in 15 seconds.

Lightly dust the saveloy sausages with extra flour, then dip into the batter. Allow any excess to drip off back into the batter from one end of the sausage — this is important for getting the textbook rounded shape on the top. Cook in small batches for 5 minutes, or until the batter is crisp and golden, and the saveloy is hot all the way through. Drain on paper towels and sprinkle with sea salt. Serve with tomato sauce, for dipping the rounded tips into.

STICK 'EM UP! *If you can find those sticks you see in toffee apples, you can insert them into the less rounded end of the saveloy before frying them one at a time.*

Pineapple & banana fritters

While these two fruity fritters were once the only dessert offerings at fish and chip shops around the nation, my fondest memory of them was from the local drive-in outdoor movie theatre. I'm not sure whether the drive-in actually sold them, or whether we bought fish and chips on the way to eat during the movie. Where we bought them wasn't exactly my focus — it was the way we enjoyed them, together as a family, watching a movie, in our car! Those nights provided many happy moments for me. Where did all those drive-ins go, anyway? They'd just about disappeared from Sydney by the time I was dating... so ripped off! No sweets with my sweetheart at the drive-in.

I've added a little spice and coconut to the batter, but feel free to omit these. I also suggest serving the fritters with Rum & raisin ice cream (page 84) and drizzled with Caramel syrup (page 217). And eating them while watching a movie at home. Now *that* I can do with my love — or on my own!

Makes 6 fritters

mild-flavoured oil, for deep-frying

110 g (3¾ oz/¾ cup) plain (all-purpose) flour

20 g (¾ oz/¼ cup) shredded coconut

½ teaspoon ground cinnamon

½ teaspoon ground ginger

a pinch of ground cardamom (optional)

¼ teaspoon caster (superfine) sugar

a pinch of sea salt

200 ml (7 fl oz) cold soda water (club soda) or sparkling mineral water

6 half-moons of fresh, ripe juicy pineapple, each 1.5 cm (⅝ inch) thick (see Note), or 3 bananas, peeled and cut in half lengthways

caster (superfine) sugar, for sprinkling (optional)

One-third fill a deep-fryer or large heavy-based saucepan with oil and heat to 180°C (350°F), or until a cube of bread dropped into the oil turns golden brown in 15 seconds.

Put the flour, coconut, spices, sugar and salt in a bowl. Add most of the soda water and whisk until smooth. The batter should be reasonably runny, but still thick enough to coat the fruit. If it is too thick, add a little more soda water. (The moisture content of flour can be affected by the weather.)

When the oil is hot, dip the fruit into the batter, then cook in small batches for 4–5 minutes, or until the batter is deep golden and crisp, and the fruit is just cooked through and hot. Drain on paper towel and sprinkle with a little caster (superfine) sugar, if desired.

Keep warm in a low oven while you finish cooking the remaining fritters. Serve hot.

NOTE *If your fresh pineapple is a little under-ripe, you could first cook the discs in a light Sugar syrup (page 216) in a small saucepan, to make them more tender and sweet. Cool, then drain before dipping them in the batter. Conversely, if your pineapple is particularly succulent and wet when you slice it, you might need to lightly dust it in flour before you dip in the batter. If pineapples are not in season, just use tinned, unsweetened pineapple rings instead; drain them well before dipping them in the batter.*

Chapter 6
CORNER STORE

THE PLACE YOU went to when no other shops were open and mum had run out of something and suddenly needed it! You either rode your bike or skimmed down the hill on your skatey to avoid being in the hot sun too long — plus it looked more cool than walking. The corner store provided all the essentials — and a little bit of everything else, from the Sunday papers (guess who'd get their mitts on the funnies first?!), bread, butter, milk and bikkies for coffee, to peanut butter for morning toast and, of course, tomato sauce to adorn the all-important pie (and just about anything else that stood still on the dinner plate). Yep, the corner store was your go-to place.

In my corner store you'll find syrups, sauces, spreads and pastries — everything you need to help you make the recipes in this book. All made from scratch, with no nasties.

Flavoured syrups

The syrups on pages 216–220 are great for shakes, for topping ice creams and desserts, adding to sparkling mineral water for your own home-made fizzy drinks, and even adding to coffee or milky tea drinks.

Your syrup may last a little less time or even longer than my suggested storage times, depending on your particular storage environment. If your syrup develops any mould or any odd aromas or flavours, it should be discarded.

Simple sugar syrup

Makes about 500 ml
(17 fl oz/2 cups)

250 g (9 oz) caster (superfine) sugar

Put the sugar in a saucepan. Add 250 ml (9 fl oz/1 cup) water and stir over medium–high heat until the sugar has dissolved. Bring to the boil and cook for 2 minutes.

Pour into a sterilised 500 ml (17 fl oz/2 cup) glass jar or bottle, seal tightly and leave to cool.

The syrup will keep in the fridge for up to 1 month. Use it to sweeten drinks and foods where the sugar needs to already be dissolved — some of the Ice blocks on pages 101–103, for example.

Chocolate syrup

Makes 500 ml (17 fl oz/2 cups)

330 g (11¾ oz/1½ cups) caster (superfine) sugar

100 g (3½ oz/½ cup) brown sugar

55 g (2 oz/½ cup) good-quality unsweetened
  cocoa powder

a pinch of fine sea salt

20 g (¾ oz) good-quality dark chocolate, chopped

½ teaspoon pure vanilla extract

¼ teaspoon cream of tartar

Place the sugars, cocoa powder and salt in a saucepan.
Gradually whisk in 375 ml (13 fl oz/1½ cups) water until
smooth, then stir over medium heat until the sugar
has dissolved.

Bring to the boil and keep at a boil, stirring occasionally
with a metal spoon for about 10 minutes, or until the
mixture thickens very slightly. It will still be fairly thin,
but will thicken again on cooling.

Remove from the heat, add the chocolate and vanilla
and whisk until the chocolate has completely melted.
Whisk in the cream of tartar until dissolved.

Pour into a sterilised 500 ml (17 fl oz/2 cup) glass bottle
or jar and seal while still hot. Cool to room temperature,
then refrigerate.

Store in the fridge and use within 6 months; discard
if any mould appears, or if the aroma or flavour suddenly
changes. Use in chocolate milkshakes, and for topping ice
cream and other desserts.

TARTAR TALES *Cream of tartar stops sugar
crystallising in syrups and confectionery, and
also helps stabilise egg whites.*

Caramel syrup

Makes 500 ml (17 fl oz/2 cups)

330 g (11¾ oz/1½ cups) caster (superfine) sugar

100 g (3½ oz/½ cup) brown sugar

250 ml (9 fl oz/1 cup) thin (pouring) cream

½ teaspoon pure vanilla extract

Put the sugars in a small saucepan with 125 ml (4 fl oz/
½ cup) water. Using a metal spoon, stir over medium heat
until the sugar has dissolved.

Increase the heat to high and bring to the boil, then
cook without stirring until the mixtre registers 145°C
(293°F) on a sugar thermometer, and is starting to smell
like toffee. If the syrup seems to be darker in a certain spot,
just swirl the pan gently until the colour is more even — do
not use a spoon to stir, or the mixture will crystallise.

Whisk in the cream using a long-handled, slim balloon
whisk — be careful as the mixture will bubble up and spit.
The caramel may 'seize' slightly, but it will melt into the
cream. Once the cream and caramel have merged together,
leave it to bubble away for 3 minutes more.

Remove from the heat, then stir in the vanilla. While
still hot, pour into a sterilised 500 ml (17 fl oz/2 cup) glass
bottle or jar and seal tightly. Very carefully invert the jar
and leave to cool to room temperature.

Store in the refrigerator and use within 3 months;
discard if any mould appears, or if the aroma or flavour
suddenly changes.

The caramel will firm up a little in the fridge, so run
the bottle under hot water until the caramel flows freely,
or bring to room temperature. Be careful not to stick any
implements inside the bottle once you start using it, as the
caramel can crystallise. Use in milkshakes, and for topping
ice cream and desserts.

Salted caramel sauce

Add 1–2 teaspoons fine sea salt flakes to the caramel when
you add the cream.

Caramel rum sauce

Add a tablespoon or so of rum to the caramel when you add
the cream.

Butterscotch sauce

Add 1½ tablespoons good-quality unsalted butter to the
caramel when you add the cream.

Coffee syrup

Makes 500 ml (17 fl oz/2 cups)

385 g (13¾ oz/1¾ cups) sugar

435 ml (15¼ fl oz/1¾ cups) freshly made espresso coffee

Put the sugar and coffee in a saucepan. Stir over medium–high heat with a metal spoon until the sugar has dissolved. Allow to come to the boil, then reduce the heat and simmer for about 22 minutes, or until the liquid has a slight syrupy consistency; it will thicken slightly on cooling.

Pour the hot syrup into a sterilised 500 ml (17 fl oz/2 cup) glass bottle or jar and seal tightly. Very carefully invert the jar and leave to cool to room temperature.

The syrup will keep in the fridge for up to 6 months; discard if any mould appears, or if the aroma or flavour suddenly changes.

Coffee vanilla syrup

Add 2 teaspoons pure vanilla extract to the syrup as soon as you remove it from the heat.

Coffee orange syrup

Add 2 large strips of orange zest (with no white pith) to the coffee mixture as soon as the sugar has dissolved; strain before bottling.

Brandied coffee syrup

In the last minutes of cooking, add 2 tablespoons brandy.

Spiced coffee syrup

Add 1 cinnamon stick, 1 cardamom pod and 2 cloves to the coffee mixture as soon as the sugar has dissolved; strain before bottling.

Strawberry syrup

Makes 500 ml (17 fl oz/2 cups)

385 g (13¾ oz/1¾ cups) caster (superfine) sugar

350 g (12 oz/2⅓ cups) ripe, aromatic strawberries, hulled, wiped over with a damp cloth, then chopped

¼ teaspoon cream of tartar

Put the sugar in a small saucepan with 185 ml (6 fl oz/¾ cup) water. Using a metal spoon, stir over medium heat until the sugar has dissolved.

Bring to the boil over high heat, then immediately reduce the heat and simmer for 15 minutes, or until the mixture has thickened slightly.

Add the strawberries and increase the heat until the mixture just comes to the boil, then reduce the heat back to a simmer. Using a hand-held stick blender, purée until smooth, then cook for a further 5 minutes. Remove from the heat and stir in the cream of tartar until dissolved.

Pour through a fine strainer, placed over a sterilised funnel, into a sterilised 500 ml (17 fl oz/2 cup) glass bottle or jar. Stir the contents to ensure all the liquid gets through the pulp, but don't push down on the fruit too much. Seal tightly and carefully invert the jar, then leave to cool to room temperature.

The syrup will keep in the fridge for up to 3 months; discard if any mould appears, or if the aroma or flavour suddenly changes.

Raspberry syrup

Simply replace the strawberries with the same amount of raspberries. There's no need to wipe them over, but do pick through to make sure all the fruit is fine. You may like to add a little extra sugar if your raspberries are tart.

Passionfruit syrup

Makes 500 ml (17 fl oz/2 cups)

440 g (15½ oz/2 cups) caster (superfine) sugar

160 g (5¾ oz/⅔ cup) passionfruit pulp (you'll need about 6–8 passionfruit)

¼ teaspoon cream of tartar

Put the sugar in a small saucepan with 375 ml (13 fl oz/1½ cups) water. Using a metal spoon, stir over medium heat until the sugar has dissolved.

Bring to the boil over high heat, then immediately reduce the heat to a steady simmer. Cook the mixture for 15–20 minutes, or until it has thickened slightly.

Add the passionfruit and bring back to the boil over high heat, then reduce the heat to a simmer and cook for a further 10 minutes. Remove from the heat and stir in the cream of tartar until dissolved.

Pour through a sieve, placed over a sterilised funnel, into a sterilised 500 ml (17 fl oz/2 cup) glass bottle or jar. Seal tightly and carefully invert the jar, then leave to cool to room temperature.

The syrup will keep in the fridge for up to 3 months; discard if any mould appears, or if the aroma or flavour suddenly changes.

Lime syrup

Makes 500 ml (17 fl oz/2 cups)

385 g (13¾ oz/1¾ cups) caster (superfine) sugar

185 ml (6 fl oz/¾ cup) fresh, strained lime juice

1 cm (½ inch) wide strip of lime zest, with no trace of white pith

Put the sugar in a small saucepan with 250 ml (9 fl oz/1 cup) water. Using a metal spoon, stir over medium heat until the sugar has dissolved.

Bring to the boil over high heat, then immediately reduce the heat to a steady simmer. Cook the mixture for 15–20 minutes, or until it has thickened very slightly.

Add the lime juice and lime zest. When the mixture comes back to a simmer, cook for a further 10 minutes, or until slightly syrupy; it will thicken further on cooling.

Remove from the heat, then strain through a sieve, discarding the zest. Pour into a sterilised 500 ml (17 fl oz/2 cup) glass bottle or jar. Seal tightly and carefully invert the jar, then leave to cool to room temperature.

The syrup will keep in the fridge for up to 2 months; discard if any mould appears, or if the aroma or flavour suddenly changes.

Lemon syrup

Increase the sugar to 440 g (15½ oz/2 cups), and replace the lime juice and zest with lemon juice and zest.

Orange syrup

Replace the lime juice and zest with orange juice and zest.

LIME TWIST *This elegant syrup is very refreshing mixed with plain old water, great in a soda, lime and bitters, as well as mocktails and cocktails. The fragile aromatic oils in lime do wear off over time, so if you haven't consumed this syrup within 2 months of making, you'll notice a distinct drop in flavour.*

Mint syrup

Makes 500 ml (17 fl oz/2 cups)

440 g (15½ oz/2 cups) caster (superfine) sugar
100 g (3½ oz/2 cups) chopped fresh mint

Put the sugar in a small saucepan with 250 ml (9 fl oz/1 cup) water. Using a metal spoon, stir over medium heat until the sugar has dissolved.

Bring to the boil over high heat, then reduce the heat to a steady simmer and cook for 10–12 minutes, or until the mixture has thickened slightly.

Add the mint and remove the pan from the heat. Allow to cool completely, then strain through a fine sieve, into a clean saucepan, and quickly bring to the boil.

Immediately remove from the heat and pour into a sterilised 500 ml (17 fl oz/2 cup) glass jar. Seal tightly and carefully invert the jar, then leave to cool to room temperature.

The syrup will keep in the fridge for up to 3 months; discard if any mould appears, or if the aroma or flavour suddenly changes.

MINTY COOLNESS *This super-refreshing syrup is seriously good in summer months, in a tall glass of mineral water or a fruity cocktail.*

Ginger syrup

Makes 500 ml (17 fl oz/2 cups)

300 g (10½ oz) fresh ginger, peeled
440 g (15½ oz/2 cups) caster (superfine) sugar

Finely mince the ginger in a food processor, then scrape out into a sturdy saucepan. Add the sugar and 875 ml (30 fl oz/3½ cups) water. Using a metal spoon, stir over medium–high heat until the sugar has dissolved.

Bring to the boil, then reduce the heat to a steady simmer. Cook for 60–70 minutes, or until the mixture is slightly syrupy; it will thicken further on cooling.

Strain through a fine strainer, into a clean saucepan, pressing down gently to help extract all the hot syrup. (It would be a travesty to throw all that luscious syrupy ginger pulp away, so store it in the freezer and add it to your next batch of muffins, banana bread or butter cake, or sprinkle it over your favourite ice cream from the Ice cream cabinet chapter!)

Bring the strained syrup to the boil again, then pour into a sterilised 500 ml (17 fl oz/2 cup) glass bottle or jar. Seal tightly and carefully invert the jar, then leave to cool to room temperature.

The syrup will keep in the fridge for up to 3 months; discard if any mould appears, or if the aroma or flavour suddenly changes.

Honey ginger syrup

Replace 110 g (3¾ oz/½ cup) of the sugar with honey.

Very exotique ginger spice syrup

Add half a cinnamon stick, 2 cardamom pods and 1 whole star anise to the mixture.

GINGER ZINGERS *If you're a ginger beer fan, just keep a bottle of this in the fridge and add to sparkling water. It also makes a great hot drink in winter when mixed with boiling water or tea and a strip of lemon zest.*

Peanut butter

Makes 330 g (11¾ oz/1¼ cups)

**350 g (12 oz/2½ cups) organic raw peanuts
 (with the skins already removed)**

1–1½ teaspoons sea salt flakes (optional)

1–1½ tablespoons peanut oil (optional)

Preheat the oven to 180°C (350°F). Line a tray with baking paper.

Spread the peanuts out on the baking tray. Transfer to the oven and roast for about 10 minutes, or until deeply golden and aromatic, stirring once if needed for even colour. Remove from the oven and leave to cool slightly.

Place in a food processor with the salt, if using, and process on a high speed until you have a fine meal. Scrape down the side of the bowl.

Turn the processor on again and continue processing for several minutes, or until the mixture is very smooth and almost fluid-like; the transformation is quite amazing — it seems like nothing is happening for a little bit, then whammo, peanut butter! Some peanuts are naturally more oily than others, so you will need to judge whether any additional peanut oil is necessary.

Transfer to a sterilised 310 ml (10¾ fl oz/1¼ cup) jar. Seal tightly, then store in a cool dark pantry or the refrigerator. It will keep for several months.

Nutty notions

Chunky peanut butter
Add some chopped toasted peanuts into your smooth base mixture, but note that you'll need a slightly bigger jar for storage.

Sweet peanut butter
You can lightly sweeten your peanut butter with a drizzle of honey when adding the peanut oil; a touch of pure vanilla extract or organic maple syrup added is also delicious.

Spiced peanut butter
Add a small amount of ground cinnamon, ground ginger or cardamom when grinding the roasted nuts; start with about ½ teaspoon, and then add more to suit your taste.

Go nutz!
You can use other nuts instead of peanuts; particularly good are macadamias, cashews, almonds, Brazil nuts and hazelnuts. You may need to add a little extra mild-flavoured oil if they're a little dry and don't liquefy after about 5 minutes of processing.

The black and white checkerboard 'tile' print linoleum which covered the floor of my local corner store was as faded and worn as some of my childhood memories are becoming. A somewhat comforting sweet and faintly smoky aroma permeated the miscellaneous goods that lined the wooden shelves — inevitably caused by years of stocking high-turnover lollies and tobacco, and perhaps enhanced by the grumpy old shopkeeper's instore smoking habit. On weekends the atmosphere was invigorated by the scent of fresh newspaper ink and the opportunity to spend a few cents of our pocket money.

Pastry

Savoury shortcrust pastry

Makes enough for 6 individual pie or quiche bases

300 g (10½ oz/2 cups) plain (all-purpose) flour, sifted

½ teaspoon fine sea salt

150 g (5½ oz) unsalted butter, cut into 1 cm (½ inch) dice and chilled

1½ teaspoons strained fresh lemon juice

60–80 ml (2–2½ fl oz/¼–⅓ cup) iced water

This pastry is easy to work with, and the recipe can easily be doubled.

Put the flour and salt in a food processor. Add the butter, then leave to sit for a few minutes to soften the butter slightly — but it should still be cold.

Pulse in short bursts until the mixture just forms roughish crumbs.

Combine the lemon juice and 60 ml (2 fl oz/¼ cup) of the iced water, then drizzle half the liquid over the crumbs. Pulse until the mixture just starts to clump. Drizzle with the remaining water and lemon juice mixture and pulse again until the dough just starts to cling together, adding the remaining water if needed.

Gather the dough up quickly and pat into a disc about 15 cm (6 inches) wide and 2 cm (¾ inch) thick. Cover with plastic wrap and refrigerate for a few hours, or overnight. Use as instructed in individual recipes.

Sweet shortcrust pastry

Makes enough for 6 individual sweet pies with lids

600 g (1 lb 5 oz/4 cups) plain (all-purpose) flour, sifted

½ teaspoon baking powder

a large pinch of sea salt

300 g (10½ oz) unsalted butter, diced and chilled

85 g (3 oz/⅔ cup) icing sugar mixture, sifted

80 ml (2½ fl oz/⅓ cup) iced water, plus an extra 2 teaspoons

This is a fragile, short pastry — not the easiest to work with, but it makes superb sweet pies.

Put the flour, baking powder and salt in a food processor and pulse to combine. Add the butter, then process just long enough for the mixture to form crumbs. Add the icing sugar and process just long enough to mix through.

Gradually add the iced water a little at a time, as you process in short bursts using the pulse button, until the mixture just forms small clumps — you may need a little less or more water, depending on the weather. If the clumps don't stick together when you squeeze them between your fingers, you'll need a little more water.

Tip the clumps onto a lightly floured work surface and gather into a ball. Flatten into a thick disc, but don't overhandle the pastry, or it will become tough. Wrap in plastic and chill for 30 minutes before using as instructed in individual recipes.

My pastry recipes are heavily inspired by the very generous and lovely Paul Allam and David McGuinness and their fantastic *Bourke Street Bakery* book. They sure know how to bake and, as they say, imitation is the greatest form of flattery. Thanks (I think) for increasing my obsession with great pies, and influencing me to form a relationship with sausage rolls too — damn you!

Puff pastry

Makes enough for 12 sausage rolls or 12 individual pie lids

135 g (4¾ oz) unsalted butter, cut into 1.5 cm (⅝ inch) dice, plus an extra 500 g (1 lb 2 oz) unsalted butter, chilled

675 g (1 lb 8 oz/4½ cups) plain (all-purpose) flour, sifted, plus extra for dusting

1 tablespoon fine sea salt

1 tablespoon strained fresh lemon juice

300 ml (10½ fl oz) iced water

Put the 135 g (4¾ oz) butter in a food processor with the flour and salt. Allow to sit for a few minutes, so the butter softens slightly, but it is still cold.

Pulse until the mixture crumbs and resembles sand. Combine the lemon juice and iced water and drizzle over the crumbs, then pulse a few times until the mixture comes together into a smooth dough. Gather together and pat into a disc about 15 cm (6 inches) wide and 2 cm (¾ inch) thick. Cover with plastic wrap and chill for at least 30 minutes, or leave overnight.

The next step will be to fold (laminate) your pastry with the 500 g (1 lb 2 oz) extra butter, but first you will need to remove the butter from the fridge and leave it until it becomes pliable — but it should still be cold.

Place the butter between two sheets of baking paper, then use a rolling pin to gently pound the butter into a 20 cm (8 inch) square, about 1 cm (½ inch) thick.

Remove the pastry from the fridge. Using even strokes, roll it out on a lightly floured work surface to a 20 x 40 cm (8 x 16 inch) rectangle, with the short sides left and right.

Place the butter square close to one short edge of the pastry, then fold the remaining pastry over to cover it completely. Pinch the edges of the pastry together to seal in the butter. Turn the pastry 90 degrees, then roll it away from you in even strokes until you have a 20 x 90 cm (8 x 35½ inch) rectangle.

Fold both short ends of the pastry in, to meet in the middle. Now fold one side of the pastry over to meet the other, as though you are closing a book. Look at the pastry and imagine the smoother side is the spine of the book, and the opposite side are the pages; remember this. Dust the pastry lightly with flour, wrap in plastic wrap and chill for 30 minutes.

Repeat this rolling, folding and chilling process three more times, but each time you roll, you must ensure that the 'spine' of your pastry is on your left before you start — this will ensure that your pastry is turned 90 degrees each time you roll. After the last roll, you will need to rest the pastry for 24 hours.

Use within 1 day of resting, or freeze for up to 2 months, wrapped in plastic wrap inside a snaplock bag or sealed plastic freezer-friendly container.

NOTE *To make this pastry easily, you will need a work bench or table more than 90 cm (35 inches) deep and wide. If not, you'll have to fiddle around by rolling your pastry out horizontally in front of you, rather than away from you — which is a little awkward, but can be done!*

Tomato sauce

Makes 500 ml (17 fl oz/2 cups)

1.5 kg (3 lb 5 oz) ripe tomatoes (see Note)

1 tablespoon safflower oil

1 small brown onion, very finely chopped

1 garlic clove, crushed

100 g (3½ oz/½ cup) brown sugar

125 ml (4 fl oz/½ cup) apple cider vinegar

a small pinch of ground celery seeds

a pinch of ground cloves or star anise

1 teaspoon mustard powder

1 fresh bay leaf

a pinch of cayenne pepper or chilli powder

NOTE *If tomatoes are not in season, use four 400 g (14 oz) tins of chopped tomatoes. Just keep an eye on the sauce, as you may need to adjust the cooking time slightly. If tomatoes are in season and on sale, feel free to double the recipe, although you'll need to cook it a little longer to reach the same consistency.*

Using the tip of a small sharp knife, cut a small cross in the bottom of each tomato. Place them in a large heatproof bowl and pour boiling water over to cover. Leave for about 1 minute, then drain and transfer to a bowl of iced water. When cool enough to handle, peel the skins back from the crosses and discard.

Working over a bowl to catch the drips, carefully cut the tomatoes in half, then scoop the seeds out and discard. Dice the flesh and place in a clean bowl. Strain the reserved tomato juices into the chopped tomato and set aside.

Heat the safflower oil in a large saucepan over medium–high heat. Sauté the onion for 6–8 minutes, or until lightly golden. Add the garlic and stir until fragrant. Increase the heat to high, add the tomatoes, 500 ml (17 fl oz/2 cups) water and the remaining ingredients, and stir to combine.

Bring just to the boil, then reduce the heat and simmer, stirring occasionally to ensure the mixture isn't sticking, for 3½ hours, or until the mixture is thick, rich and pulpy. Remove from the heat and allow to cool slightly.

Discard the bay leaf. Purée the mixture as smooth as possible, using a food processor or hand-held stick blender. Strain, return to a clean pan and bring back to the boil.

Strain through a sterilised funnel, staight into a sterilised 500 ml (17 fl oz/2 cup) jar or bottle. Screw the lid on tightly, then turn upside down until cool.

Store in the fridge for up to 6 months; discard if you see any sign of mould, or if the flavour suddenly changes. Serve as a condiment to meat pies, burgers, eggs or chips.

Barbecue sauce

Makes 375 ml (13 fl oz/1½ cups)

1 tablespoon safflower oil

1 small onion, very finely chopped

1 garlic clove, crushed

400 g (14 oz) tin chopped tomatoes

1 tablespoon tomato paste (concentrated purée)

60 ml (2 fl oz/¼ cup) apple cider vinegar

60 g (2¼ oz/⅓ cup) brown sugar

1 teaspoon smoked sweet paprika

1 teaspoon mustard powder

1 teaspoon ground allspice

½ teaspoon ground star anise

¼ teaspoon cayenne pepper or chilli powder

2 tablespoons worcestershire sauce

Heat the safflower oil in a saucepan over medium heat and sauté the onion for 10 minutes, or until golden. Add the garlic and stir until fragrant.

Add all the remaining ingredients, except 2 teaspoons of the worcestershire sauce. Pour in 375 ml (13 fl oz/1½ cups) water and stir until the sugar has dissolved. Bring the mixture to the boil, then reduce the heat and simmer, stirring regularly, for 1½–1¾ hours, or until the sauce has reduced and thickened slightly.

Allow to cool slightly, then purée using a hand-held stick blender or upright blender. Strain the sauce into a small clean saucepan and bring to the boil. Stir in the remaining worcestershire sauce and season to taste with sea salt and freshly ground black pepper.

Carefully pour the hot sauce into a sterilised 375 ml (13 fl oz/1½ cup) glass jar or bottle. Screw the lid on tight and turn upside down until completely cool.

Store in the fridge for up to 6 months; discard if any mould appears, or if the flavour suddenly changes. Use as a condiment for burgers, barbecued meats, bacon and eggs.

Chilli sauce

Makes 330 ml (11¼ fl oz/1⅓ cups)

1 large red capsicum (pepper)

6 long red chillies

4 small very hot red chillies

1 small brown onion, chopped

2 garlic cloves, chopped

125 ml (4 fl oz/½ cup) apple cider vinegar

1 tablespoon lemon juice

1 teaspoon smoked sweet paprika

a pinch of ground cloves

3 teaspoons sea salt

2 tablespoons brown sugar

SOME LIKE IT HOT! *This sauce is medium hot. If you yearn for the burn, add a few more small hot chillies.*

Remove the stems, seeds and any white membrane from the capsicum and chillies. Roughly chop the capsicum and chillies and place in a food processor. Add all the remaining ingredients, except the sugar. Pour in 375 ml (13 fl oz/1½ cups) water and process until the mixture is as smooth as possible.

Scrape the mixture into a saucepan, add the sugar and stir well. Bring to the boil over high heat, then reduce to a simmer. Cook, stirring regularly to ensure the mixture doesn't stick to the pan, for about 2 hours, or until the mixture is thick but still pourable.

Remove from the heat, leave to cool slightly, then purée until smooth using an upright blender or hand-held stick blender. Pass through a sieve, into a clean saucepan, and bring just to the boil.

Carefully pour through a sterilised funnel, into a sterilised 330 ml (11¼ fl oz/1⅓ cup) glass jar or bottle. Screw the lid on tight and turn upside down until completely cool.

Store the sauce in the fridge for up to 6 months; discard if any mould appears, or if the aroma or flavour suddenly changes.

Satay sauce

Makes 375 ml (13 fl oz/1½ cups)

1½ tablespoons peanut oil

1 small red onion, finely chopped

2 garlic cloves, crushed

1 teaspoon grated fresh ginger

2 teaspoons ground cumin

½ teaspoon ground coriander

½ teaspoon ground cinnamon

2 tablespoons finely chopped fresh coriander (cilantro) root

1 lemongrass stem, white part only, bruised

125 g (4½ oz/½ cup) chopped tinned tomatoes

2 tablespoons Chilli sauce (page 228) or ready-made chilli sauce

400 ml (14 fl oz) tin coconut cream

140 g (5 oz/½ cup) Peanut butter (page 221) or ready-made peanut butter

1 tablespoon brown sugar

3 teaspoons lime juice

2 teaspoons fish sauce

Heat the peanut oil in a large saucepan over medium–high heat. Add the onion and sauté for 10 minutes, or until golden. Add the garlic, ginger and ground spices and stir until fragrant.

Add the coriander root, lemongrass stem, tomatoes, chilli sauce and coconut cream and bring to the boil. Reduce the heat to a simmer and cook for 40 minutes.

Remove the lemongrass, then stir in the peanut butter and sugar. Cook for a further 10 minutes, stirring regularly to stop the mixture sticking. Stir in the lime juice and fish sauce and season to taste with sea salt.

Pour the hot sauce into a sterilised 375 ml (13 fl oz/ 1½ cup) glass jar or bottle. Screw the lid on tight and turn upside down until completely cool.

Store in the fridge and use within 2 weeks. You can also freeze half if you don't think you will use all the sauce within that time.

Tartare sauce

Makes about 250 g (9 oz/1 cup)

165 g (5¾ oz/⅔ cup) Mayonnaise (page 231)
or good-quality ready-made mayonnaise

1½ tablespoons very finely chopped white onion,
squeezed to extract any liquid

2 tablespoons salted capers, rinsed well and
finely chopped

2 small sweet, spiced gherkins or dill pickles,
finely chopped

1 garlic clove, crushed

1½–2 teaspoons finely chopped fresh tarragon

1½ tablespoons finely chopped flat-leaf
(Italian) parsley

3 teaspoons good-quality white wine vinegar

2 teaspoons dijon mustard

Simply place all the ingredients in a small non-metallic bowl and mix together well. Cover and refrigerate for at least 2 hours before serving, to allow the flavours to develop. Store in the fridge and use within 1 week.

This sauce goes well with many of the seafood recipes in the Fish 'n' Chip Shop chapter.

Cocktail sauce
(AKA MARIE ROSE SAUCE)

Makes about 185 g (6½ oz/¾ cup)

120 g (4¼ oz/½ cup) Mayonnaise (page 231)
or good-quality ready-made mayonnaise

1½ tablespoons Tomato sauce (page 226) or
store-bought tomato sauce (ketchup)

3 teaspoons horseradish cream

1 teaspoon worcestershire sauce

1 teaspoon lemon juice

a few drops of Tabasco sauce

Simply place all the ingredients in a small non-metallic bowl and mix together well. Cover and refrigerate for at least 1 hour before serving, to allow the flavours to develop. Store in the fridge and use within 1 week.

This sauce is the quintessential prawn (shrimp) cocktail dressing; toss with cooked peeled prawns and serve with lettuce and avocado for a quick prawn cocktail.

Mayonnaise

Makes 235 g (8½ oz/1 cup)

2 large egg yolks, at room temperature

1 tablespoon lemon juice

2 teaspoons good-quality white wine vinegar or apple cider vinegar

1½ teaspoons dijon mustard

a large pinch of sugar

½ teaspoon fine sea salt

a pinch of ground white pepper

2 tablespoons extra virgin olive oil

125 ml (4 fl oz/½ cup) mild-flavoured vegetable oil, such as sunflower or safflower

Put the egg yolks, lemon juice, vinegar, mustard, sugar, salt and pepper in a blender, or the bowl of an electric mixer fitted with a whisk attachment. Mix until well combined.

Combine the oils. While continually whisking or blending at medium–high speed, gradually add the oils to the egg yolk — just a fine drizzle at first, until the mixture starts to come together, then you can add the oil in a steadier flow and increase the speed of the whisking. You should end up with a thick, creamy mayonnaise.

Season to taste with a little more salt, if needed. Store in a sterile glass jar in the fridge and use within 1 week.

Aïoli (garlic mayonnaise)

Grind 5 garlic cloves to a paste with a little sea salt using a mortar and pestle, or finely chop together using a sharp, heavy knife. Add the garlic paste to the egg mixture at the point above when you first start to mix, omitting the mustard if you wish. (You can also replace the vinegar with extra lemon juice, or vice versa if you prefer.) Store in a sterile jar in the fridge and use within a few days.

INDEX

ACKNOWLEDGEMENTS

There are always so many people to thank on a book project — far more than you could possibly imagine.

Firstly thank you to Diana Hill, Sue Hines and the team at Murdoch Books for once again allowing me to put some stuff on pages to send out into the world.

Thank you to all the editorial and design staff who keep things ticking, ask all the right questions and polish up the stuff I put on pages to turn it into a book: Virginia Birch, Katri Hilden, Hugh Ford, Clare O'Loughlin, David Potter and Emma Hutchinson.

Of course, without gorgeous recipe shots, a food book can present as a little dull... so thanks for making it sing Brett Stevens, Maree Homer, Matt Page, Louise Bickle, Heidi Moore and Grace Campbell. Oh, and thanks for the seagulls...

To all those fabulous food people who helped me test and perfect all my recipes: I literally could not have done this without you. Rozzie Baldwin, Lou Bell Barrett, Stephanie Clifford Smith, Gerard Kambeck, Peta Dent, Jill Brand and Gabriela Oporto — you all completely rock!

Thanks always to my family and friends for lending me their palates during the testing phase, and for always supporting and understanding when my head is immersed in book-land and deadlines. Thank you GG for playing chauffeur for the many, sadly washed-out, photography road trips... oh the joy.

And thank you to YOU for buying this book! I hope you enjoy it as much as I enjoyed making it.

Published in 2016 by Murdoch Books, an imprint of Allen & Unwin

Murdoch Books Australia
83 Alexander Street
Crows Nest NSW 2065
Phone: +61 (0) 2 8425 0100
Fax: +61 (0) 2 9906 2218
murdochbooks.com.au
info@murdochbooks.com.au

Murdoch Books UK
Ormond House
26-27 Boswell Street
London WC1N 3JZ
Phone: +44 (0) 20 8785 5995
murdochbooks.co.uk
info@murdochbooks.co.uk

For Corporate Orders & Custom Publishing contact Noel Hammond, National Business
Development Manager, Murdoch Books Australia

Publisher: Diana Hill
Project Manager: Emma Hutchinson
Editor: Katri Hilden
Cover design: Madeleine Kane
Internal design concept: Clare O'Loughlin
Internal design layout: Transformer
Photographers: Brett Stevens and Maree Homer
Stylists: Matt Page and Louise Bickle
Home Economists: Heidi Moore and Grace Campbell
Production Manager: Alexandra Gonzalez